Death Without Fear

Also by Harvey Humann
The Many Faces of Angels
DeVorss & Co., Marina del Rey, California

". . . an awakening experience!"

"A changing attitude towards death is one of the major phenomena of our age. Although many people are still saddled with an essentially medieval view of death, we are experiencing a spiritual awakening. Of course, the sheath or bodily vehicle, which enables us to operate on the material plane, must be discarded when the time is ripe. [But this does nothing to change the fact that] we are immortal spiritual beings, droplets of Divinity and Life, which cannot possibly die. This understanding involves a veritable turn-about in the center of our consciousness.

"Death Without Fear is one of the best possible books for awakening the reader to the true picture of the immortal soul's passage through embodiment in the School of Earth. It is a splendid, clear and precise statement, which will help many to face death with joy, anticipation and courage. Nothing could be more important and vital for our time than the contents of this book. Harvey Humann has made a fine contribution to the spiritual awakening of our time."

Sir George Trevelyan,
Author of *A Vision of the Aquarian Age*

"Harvey Humann convincingly presents findings of paranormal research to support his belief that death is not the end of life, but rather a transition to an even fuller life. Whether facing one's own death, or grieving over the death of a loved one, *Death Without Fear* will be a source of great comfort and strength."

Ruth Mattson Taylor,
Editor of *Witness From Beyond*

"This book is an awakening experience! *Death Without Fear* is a clearly written and well-researched gem of a book. Harvey Humann summarizes and organizes the best research available on living and dying. I can think of nothing that better frees me (or anybody else) from fear and anxiety than spiritual perspectives concerning the final passage of life."

Jean K. Foster,
Writer of *The God-Mind Connection*

"Harvey Humann's book *Death Without Fear* reviews the mystical literature in a concise and efficacious manner that lends substance to his hypothesis that the term 'death' may really be misnomer."

Fowler C. Jones, Ed.D.,
Associate Professor in Psychiatry,
University of Kansas Medical Center

"In sharing their dying experiences, my hospice patients have taught me that we are more than our physical bodies, that existence does not cease when our physical body no longer functions and we do not die alone. Harvey Humann's book, *Death Without Fear,* offers explanations for these experiences .

"The religious and the traditionalists may jump on *Death Without Fear* negatively, the mentalists may debate its validity, but the grieving and the suffering may ponder it and find comfort. Since you can only please some of the people some of the time, what a wonderful group to affect."

Barbara Karnes, RN,
Director of Hospice and Home Health Services of Olathe Medical Center
and author of *GONE FROM MY SIGHT - The Dying Experience* and *MY FRIEND, I CARE - The Grief Experience*

Death Without Fear

by

Harvey Humann

PENTHE Publishing Co.
Lawrence, Kansas

Permissions

Penthe Publications wishes to express its gratitude for permission to use copyright material to Paul Beard and Pilgrim Books for excerpts from *Living On, Hidden Man* and *The Barbanell Report*; to The College of Psychic Studies for extracts from *Letters from our Daughters, Part I, Sally* by Rosamond Lehmann, quotations by Kathleen Raine from *Light* Magazine, for passages from the *Other World (C.P.S. Paper No. 7)* by Albert Pauchard; to the Swedenborg Foundation, Inc. for permission to use a passage from *Heaven and Hell* by Emanuel Swedenborg; to Hodder & Stoughton, Limited for the use of extracts from *The Imprisoned Splendour, Nurslings of Immortality, Watchers on the Hill, The Light and the Gate* and *A Pool of Reflections,* by Raynor C. Johnson; to the Edgar Cayce Foundation for quoted material from a lecture and a reading by Edgar Cayce; to Sigo Press for a passage from *A Vision of the Aquarian Age* by Sir George Trevelyan; to Random House, Inc., for the use of passages from the Vintage Books Edition of *The Doctor and the Soul* by Viktor Frankl; to Foreword Books for permission to use excerpts from *Witness From Beyond,* edited by Ruth Mattson Taylor; to the C.W. Daniel Co. for the use of passages from *Testimony of Light* by Helen Greaves; to the C.W. Daniel Co. and The Chalice Well Trust for their kind permission to use material from *The Silent Road* by W. Tudor Pole; to The White Eagle Publishing Trust for the use of quoted material from *The Return of Arthur Conan Doyle* by Ivan Cooke; to William Morrow and Company for the use of extracts from *Heading Toward Omega* by Kenneth Ring; to the Radha Soami Satsang Beas Publishing Company for a passage from *Yoga and the Bible* by Joseph Leeming.

A work of this nature is necessarily dependent on material taken from numerous sources. Some of the sources quoted in *Death Without Fear* are by now considerably dated and it has been impossible to ascertain in every case whether a particular passage is taken from a copyright work. If we have unknowingly infringed upon copyright in any way, we offer our sincere apology and would be thankful for information which would allow us to make appropriate acknowledgement in future editions.

ISBN: 0-9632475-6-5
Library of Congress Card Catalog
Number: 92-80778

PENTHE Publishing Co.

P.O. Box 994 * Lawrence, KS 66044-0994
U.S.A.

Printed in the United States of America

In Honor of
Paul Beard

In Memory of
Raynor Johnson
&
Hugh Lynn Cayce

Acknowledgements

Many people have helped to make this book a reality. We would like to express our heartfelt gratitude to all who have contributed, most especially to Carl and Jean Foster for sharing their publishing experience and to David and Mary Dohrmann for well-timed networking, to Ursula Gilkeson, whose hours of trial and error resulted in the cover design, to Diane Silver for a dose of confidence when it was most needed and to Paul Beard, and Ruth Mattson Taylor for the kind help they have given to this project.

The cover painting is "Temple of Life - Center of Our Consciousness" by the Russian visionary artist Viacheslav Petrov-Gladky. In the pre-*glasnost* Soviet Union, at a time when art with spiritual content was suppressed, he was known as the "master of unsanctioned art." A native of Moscow, Mr. Petrov-Gladky now lives and works in Frankfurt, Germany.

For more information about the work of Viacheslav Petrov-Gladky, contact Penthe Publishing Company.

Table of Contents

PREFACE

THERE WAS A TIME when most of our assumptions about death and the afterlife could go unchallenged by information. Actually *examining* what we believe about what happens after death in the light of what is actually known on the subject has never seemed to be an option that is open to most of us.

But times change, often faster than we do. Investigation into the phenomena surrounding what is termed "near-death experience," in which a person who has been declared clinically dead makes a comeback, has verified that something indeed happens after physical death. Persons who have had a near-death experience are afterward able to report on at least the preliminary stages of the death process. There are now thousands of recorded cases of the near-death experience. They are well documented in clinical research and have been corroborated so thoroughly that we now have something approaching a consensus picture of what that experience entails. We are still free to believe that life ends with physical death, of course, but there is now abundant evidence to the contrary.

If the phenomenon of the near-death experience has gained a certain cautious acceptance in some scientific circles, no such bridge has yet been built between conventional understanding of life and death processes and the findings of organized afterlife research. This research has been carried on since the 1880's, most notably in England,

11

but the results do not often fit comfortably into systems of thought which insist on objectifiable evidence.

In its usual form, afterlife research involves the study of reports by persons who claim to have communications from the deceased. This obviously poses many significant problems when it comes to talking seriously about these subjects and people who blithely assume that the general public is (or should be) ready to accept this type of information uncritically are blessed with an astonishing amount of naïveté. We must acknowledge that there is a tremendous gap between these reports and the everyday life of most people. Communications about the afterlife come from sources which most people cannot verify and from "places" to which there is not ready access. Therefore, those who want to look into the results of afterlife research may have to prepare themselves for being called "unscientific." It remains to be seen, however, whether this is more a statement about afterlife research or about the limitations of science.

Authentic afterlife researchers are not crackpots. They are no less eager to get to the truth of the matter than are authentic physicists or authentic biologists. They are well aware that a statement is not valid - or invalid - simply because it happens to come from a discarnate source and in the more than one hundred years of collection, categorization and analysis of this kind of material, great care has been taken to separate the wheat from the chaff. Still, whether one takes those reports seriously or not is obviously very strongly linked to personal experience and, as with any field of endeavor that moves us out beyond our normal thinking about the way things are, an open mind is essential.

The unique angle of *Death Without Fear* is that in it Harvey Humann gives the reader an undogmatic look at this accumulation of information and an introduction to some of the most reliable contributors to this field. In this book, he places a survey of the clinical findings about the near-death experience alongside a sampling of the less well-known but equally self-consistent and voluminous testimonies of mystics and mediums about the afterlife.

As in any specialized field, a considerable amount of jargon has developed over the years among students of afterlife research. In *Death Without Fear*, we have dispensed with these conventions wherever they may have stood in the way of clarity for the reader who may be making his or her first foray into this subject matter. The quoted material has not been altered, however, and in a number of places, some of the language peculiar to afterlife research and discarnate communication will be in evidence.

The annotated bibliography in the back of the book includes background information about the sources of quoted material.

James Gilkeson, Editor

"On Earth, the broken arcs,
In Heaven a perfect round,
All we have willed or hoped
Or dreamed of good,
Shall exist."

Robert Browning

FOREWORD
by Audrey F. Humann

MY HUSBAND, HARVEY HUMANN, received an unexpected diagnosis of terminal cancer just two months before his death in October of 1990. He had completed the manuscript of this book four months earlier.

I think it might be significant to the reader to know that he accepted his diagnosis very beautifully, even though it came as a complete surprise. He replied to the doctor, "That's OK. I am ready. Just let me die at home and keep me as pain-free as possible." Because he believed so deeply in all he has expressed in this book, he was an inspiration to his family, his doctors, nurses and everyone with whom he spoke.

Harvey did not achieve his spiritual beliefs all at once; they evolved over a period of thirty years of study and research. Although he began with an interest in parapsychology, he soon lost interest in psychic demonstrations and chose to follow the path of spiritual growth and the working of the Universal Law of cause and effect. He concluded that mankind's purpose in physical life was to express love and service.

He tried to follow these principles in his business life, his community, his church and his family. As a result, he was loved by all who knew him. He knew he had a long journey of perhaps many lifetimes to achieve spiritual perfection and felt it was the destiny of each of us to choose our own pathway. He anticipated opportunities for further spiritual growth through love and service on the astral level. His beliefs gave serenity to his life and to his death.

Death Without Fear has been a labor of love for all who have been involved with it. Our daughter, Ann Hedrick, has been a great source of loving support and encouragement at all times during the book's preparation and our best proof-reader and critic. The book went from a complete, though unedited, manuscript to a finished publication mainly through the abilities and efforts of editor and publisher James Gilkeson, who took on responsibility for all phases of the project.

It is my hope that this book will give the reader peace of mind when thinking of the close of this phase of life.

A PERSONAL NOTE FROM PAUL BEARD

Author of *Hidden Man* and *Living On* and
former President of the College of Psychic Studies, London

THE MANY APPROACHES to the problem of whether we do indeed survive death often represent judgments which have their basis within the parameters of other disciplines. It is a very different matter to find one's own private evidence, to evaluate it and then - most importantly - to be willing to incorporate its meanings within the patterns of daily living. This requires acts of self committal. The evidence of the survival of bodily death is complex, with shallows to be detected and avoided. At its best, however, it is powerful. The most important part lies beyond merely recognizing the minds and feelings of those dear to us who are convincingly in contact with us, for they go on to tell us much of new disciplines and the serious intent needed to work on their limitations before they can reach rich tapestries of living further along the road.

It is this inner area which Harvey Humann explores and recounts with the total integrity, humility and depth of being which characterized his own life. That which he came to accept as valuable and true he then put into practice, especially in his years of hospice work. He learned how to live alike for the present and the future. The fruit of his many years of earnest searching for truth, which he offers in this book, cannot fail to be found of much worth.

INTRODUCTION
by Harvey Humann

AS A HOSPICE VOLUNTEER, I discovered a tragic lack of knowledge among patients about life after death. In most cases, they quietly held on to a few vague beliefs about heaven, but they had only the slightest notion of what they might actually *do* when they got there. The result in most of these persons was fear and undue suffering at the time of the greatest transition they will ever know in their earthly lives.

It is regrettable that these patients and their families are either unaware of or not interested in the vast body of literature on the afterlife. Together with the more widely known studies of cases in which persons who have been clinically dead and then have been revived, a picture forms which is both consistent and compelling. One can emerge from a sincere study of this literature with the conviction that the soul survives death and that death is a birth into a new, yet unlived life.

In the last twenty years, I have discovered a number of authors who speak with authority and credibility of the "many mansions in God's house," a heaven filled with endless duties, responsibilities and opportunities, where we can continue to grow in knowledge and spiritual understanding. For this book, I have selected ten of these authors and seers who stand apart from others by virtue of their wide range of knowledge of the next world's many different levels.

I am especially indebted to three of these teachers in particular, all personal friends, who have added much to my understanding of the next world. One of them is Paul Beard, author, well-known psychical researcher and one of England's leading authorities on the nature of the next world. The second is Hugh Lynn Cayce, 1907-1982, son of the gifted teacher, Edgar Cayce, the first to make me clearly aware that we have had many previous lifetimes on Earth. For thirty years he was the spiritual and intellectual leader of the Association for Research and Enlightenment, the Edgar Cayce Foundation.

Finally, I would like to single out Raynor Johnson, a scientist, philosopher and teacher whose critical mind and wide learning brought me to a new understanding of man's role in the universe. In the fifteen years of our acquaintance, I was continually impressed with his deep sincerity and spiritual integrity. Johnson wrote on spiritual and mystical subjects with a clear, intellectual style and authority and his spiritual insights and unpretentious authority made him a well known figure in the field of psychical research.

Death Without Fear is a response to those who find themselves in need of information about what happens after death. I have attempted to bring together the best-known material about the near-death experience and place it alongside what I believe to be the best and most authoritative descriptions of the afterlife, gathered from direct sources. If anything is to be gained from these descriptions of the afterlife, it is the solace that comes from the testimony of those who have gone on ahead of us into unknown territory and then returned with a report of what lies before us. It is my sincere wish that this book will bring comfort to the reader.

Chapter One

Death and Near-Death

GLIMPSES OF THE NEXT WORLD

OUR SOCIETY has a complex about death, the great enigma which we have perpetually feared, ignored and misunderstood, but never eliminated. Death reminds us of our own mortal limits and our reluctance to talk about it shows how concerned we really are.

All of us have an unexpressed need to know how and where we survive when our body dies. But because we are a busy people, immersed in life's daily pressures and trivia, we seldom give serious thought to this unanswered question. From time to time, however, when a friend or loved one dies, we are reminded of our own mortality and uncertain final destination.

Death is as much a part of human life as birth. It gives meaning to our existence by setting a limit to the time we have on this Earth. Rightly understood, death can instill us with a new sense of urgency and the need to do something worthwhile with the time that is ours. It can gently remind us to not wait until next year or next month, or even tomorrow to begin to love more, show more kindness and more fully appreciate life and everything around us. Many people, when suddenly confronted with impending death, are filled with a new reverence for life. They see beauty that had escaped them before. They have - as never before - a new sense of loving, caring and even forgiving.

We cannot deny the pain caused by the death of someone we love deeply. It is a time of physical separation, a time of deep, private grief and sadness. The knowledge, however, that consciousness continues, that death is only a passage into a new world, can mitigate the intensity of pain and sorrow.

Belief in the soul's survival after death is the principal tenet of faith in all great religious traditions. In the context of mankind's long history, *disbelief* in survival is but a brief modern aberration caused by the tenuous intellectual assumption that science is the sole source of truth and that no evidence is admissible if it is not quantifiable or if it takes the psyche or the non-physical world into consideration. Materialists may limit reality to what the physical senses perceive, but their arguments are losing their ability to convince as serious research ventures into questions of what lies beyond this life.

NEAR DEATH EXPERIENCES

There are now many recorded instances of patients who have been pronounced clinically dead, only to return from that state and share what they have experienced. These reports are filled with depictions of a brilliant, beautiful world. For many, skepticism and cynicism on the part of their listeners cut short the telling of their exciting story. They are often told, in effect, to take a valium and get some rest. Or it is suggested that they have had a hallucination during their brief period of unconsciousness. Whether they are believed or not, however, after near-death experiences of the kind described in this book, these patients never fear death again because they know where they are going and what they are going to see. Their whole outlook on life changes dramatically.

In recent years, medical science has taken an interest in this phenomenon and a growing number of books have been written about the near-death experience. A handful of doctors and psychiatrists have studied the testimonies of hundreds of patients who have glimpsed the next world. The names of Raymond Moody, Michael Sabom, Elisabeth Kübler-Ross and Kenneth Ring are now well-known in thanatological research, the scientific inquiry into death and dying. They have found that many patients who previously were reluctant to speak of their experiences for fear of ridicule and skepticism are now willing to share their stories.

Dr. Raymond Moody's book, *Life After Life*, reports on his study of 150 men and women of all ages who revived after suffering apparent death. These patients came from widely diverse national, racial and religious backgrounds. The overlapping of the descriptions of their near-death experiences are so striking that they are difficult, if not impossible, to explain away as mere coincidences.

Dr. Michael Sabom, Cardiologist and Professor of Medicine at Emery University, verified many of Moody's findings. Over a five year period he interviewed 116 patients and published his findings in *Recollections of*

Death: A Medical Investigation. From interviews he conducted with patients, he found a pattern emerging in which he identified two stages which were passed through - always in the same sequence - by *all* of his subjects.

He called the first stage the *autoscopic stage,* in which the patient saw everything in the room from a point outside of his or her physical body.

Perhaps more than any other near-death researcher, Dr. Sabom found striking evidence that patients who had cardiac arrests on the operating table and in intensive care units had the experience of observing themselves from a point outside their physical bodies during their near-death experience. One patient was able to pinpoint the exact position from which he viewed his body. Dr. Sabom theorizes that during a near-death crisis the mind and brain separate, and the mind continues to function outside of the physical body.

The second stage of the near-death experience is called the *transcendental stage* by Sabom. Patients reported seeing themselves moving down a dark tunnel and suddenly coming upon a great light in which they saw people who had died recently. Others heard voices that told them to go back because it was not yet their time, whereupon they suddenly found themselves back in their bodies. His conclusion was that the physical brain and the non-physical mind are separate and distinct from one another.

Dr. Elisabeth Kübler-Ross has written more books than anyone else on the subject of death and dying. In her lectures and writings, she talks at great length about the life-changing insights of many persons who pass through

24

near-death experiences. Her work has brought her into contact with innumerable terminally ill patients in all parts of the world. Time and time again, the universality of the autoscopic and transcendental features of the near-death experience is corroborated. Patients emerge from these experiences with an awareness that death does not really exist. They experience the shedding of their physical body in a process often likened to a butterfly moving out of its cocoon. They describe a transition into another level of consciousness where they continue to perceive, to understand and to grow. The overwhelming consensus is that the only thing we lose in death is the physical body.

Dr. Ross tells the story of a patient who had been in and out of intensive care fifteen times. No one expected her to survive these crises, but she always managed to pull through. During one crisis, she was in a private room, very close to death. She could not decide whether or not to call a nurse because she knew she had only a few minutes to live. One part of her wanted very much for the transition to come, but another part wanted to make it just one more time because she felt that her youngest son was still too young. Before she could make up her mind, though, a nurse happened to look in on her and dashed out to get help. At that moment the woman felt herself moving out of her physical body and floating three or four feet above her bed. It surprised her to see how pale her body was where it lay on the bed. And yet, she was completely conscious, both of her own thoughts and of everything going on around her. The resuscitation team rushed into the room and went to work on her body. From her vantage point

25

she could see who came into the room first, who came in last and what they were wearing. She even remembered a joke that one of the interns told to relieve the tension. She remembered talking to the resuscitation team from her position above her body and telling them to calm down. Three and a half hours later she made a comeback and lived another year and a half.

Independent studies by Dr. Kenneth Ring, Professor of Psychology at the University of Connecticut, have served to further document the near-death experience and present a more differentiated picture of its features. His book, *Heading Toward Omega*, represents a milestone in the research of the near-death experience. After interviewing hundreds of patients with near-death experiences, Dr. Ring found that most of these had these five core experiences:

1. A sense of well-being; patients described the first stage as a feeling of total peace, beauty and all-pervading love, an ecstasy of freedom and a release from pain.

2. The sensation of separating from the body; accompanied by a clear awareness of everything that was happening around them.

3. Passage through a dark tunnel and a feeling of motion; often, the point is made that no fear is felt at this stage.

4. An encounter with a bright light and feelings of peace and warmth.

5. Entering the light itself; patients speak of their entry into a world of light where they experience a sense of "other-worldliness," of overwhelming beauty. It is at this stage that they see loved ones who have died earlier and are waiting to greet them. They see beautiful landscapes, trees, flowers and hear sublime music. Some say they were reluctant to return from this peaceful, beautiful world that resembles paradise.

> Suddenly I found myself in the most beautiful country . . . the color was unlike anything on Earth. The whole scene was bathed in a beautiful, energizing light. In the distance I could see a river and there was someone on the other side. I didn't want to leave. . . . I saw my parents approach me. They seemed not at all surprised to see me. In fact, they looked as though they were waiting for me and expecting me. . . . Suddenly, somebody, possibly my father, communicated to me that I must go back, I could not stay, as it was not my time and I still had much to do. So I must return.

Throughout his research, Ring consistently found that the near-death experience tended to lead to "an unassailable conviction that there is life after death." His patients often reported dramatic and permanent changes in their way of viewing life as a result of the insight that their experience would continue even after their physical death. One patient echoed the certainty expressed by all of Dr. Ring's patients.

> I know there is life after death! Nobody can shake my belief. I have no doubt - it's peaceful and nothing to be feared. I don't know what's beyond what I've experienced, but it's plenty for me. . . . I only know that death is not to be feared, only dying.

When we realize how much of our lives is unconsciously dictated by the fear of death, it is not difficult at all to understand the positive and sometimes radical changes which occur in the lifestyles of persons who have had a near-death experience. In the chapters to follow, we will examine depictions of what follows physical death, offered by recognized authorities in the field of afterlife research. In these depictions, a cogent picture of the soul's survival and afterlife emerges, which, if understood, can bring about a revolution in our notions of life and death.

Chapter Two

Survival and Seven Stages
of Transition

*"Thy guru has set thee before the clear light and now thou art
about to experience it in reality."*
      Tibetan Book of the Dead, The Bardo Thödol

BEYOND THE NEAR-DEATH
EXPERIENCE

COMFORTING as documented study of the near-death
experience of those who have returned from death's
doorstep may be, where do we turn for evidence of what
lies *beyond* these wonderful and life-changing experiences?
They are, after all, *near*-death experiences and, as such,
only intimations of things to come. Is there more?

To examine what is known about life after the
completed death experience, we have at least three major
sources which can be drawn upon. One is the historical
depictions of heaven which make up a significant part of
the traditions and articles of faith of most religions.
Another source is statements by mystics who claim that a
vision of the afterlife has been revealed to them. The third
great source of information is the cumulative testimony of
persons endowed with extraordinary psychic sensitivity
who at times make telepathic contact with the minds of

those who have gone through physical death and wish to communicate about their experiences. This third category of information will make up the bulk of the rest of this book.

It is important to bear in mind that real *proof* of survival is a very elusive and personal thing. What may constitute absolute proof for some may not be that at all for others. Many people believe in survival and the immortality of the soul. But believing is still one step away from actually *knowing*. At the approach of death, many will still have lingering doubts about survival. In the words of Paul Beard, "Intellectual proof alone [of survival] always has one missing ingredient and that is the response that must come from within us. This can only come if we are able to cultivate it for ourselves."

The implication here is that we must use the tools of faith, prayer and meditation in order to come into a clear awareness that we are spiritual, immortal beings. In spite of all the evidence that we may see and hear, we still have to cultivate our own faith about this business of survival. In the following, we will endeavor to portray the afterlife using a variety of testimonies from both the past and present.

HISTORICAL DEPICTIONS
OF HEAVEN

A guidebook of heaven of the first millennium of the Christian era would have been a relatively simple replica of the Garden of Eden, a pastoral paradise of hills, valleys, streams and lakes, trees and flowers, a place of Eternal Rest. This popular image began to change in the Middle Ages. In the two centuries between 1100 and 1300 A.D., the number of cities in central Europe grew from 200 to 1500. This demographic change brought with it a gradual migration of monks from the countryside and villages to the cities. This shifted the center of religious influence and religious teaching from rural churches to urban centers. The priestly community who previously taught that heaven was a simple nature-paradise now began to describe heaven as the Holy City, resplendent with pearly gates, walls and streets paved with gold and jasper. Of course, they found ample biblical endorsement for these notions in John's Revelation.

> Her light was like unto a stone, most precious. Even like a jasper stone, clear as a crystal; and had a wall great and high, and had twelve gates and at the gates twelve angels. . . . And the city lieth foursquare, and the length is as large as the breadth: and he measured the city with the reed, twelve thousand furlongs. . . .
>
> And the twelve gates were twelve pearls; every several gate was of one pearl: and the street of the city was pure gold, as it were transparent glass. (Rev. 21:11,12,16,21)

In this depiction of heaven, the Heavenly City was presided over by Christ surrounded by choirs of angels and a retinue of prophets, patriarchs, martyrs and apostles. To help Christians identify with the splendor of the Heavenly City, medievalists built their cities around majestic Gothic cathedrals to bring to Earth a replica of heaven.

An estimated 80 cathedrals were built throughout Christendom between 1170 and 1270. These magnificent edifices were the skyscrapers of their day. Their art, sculptures, gold vessels and chalices, their pageantry and liturgy combined to transport the faithful to a City of Heaven which was not of this Earth.

This popular concept of heaven prevailed until the Renaissance, which ushered in the concept of a two-tiered heaven. The upper tier was occupied by Christ's Holy Family, the lower tier was a vast natural landscape teeming with common people busy with endless activities, unconcerned about what was happening above. Some artists pictured the two tiers connected by Jacob's ladder.

A EUROPEAN VISIONARY

In the middle of the 18th century a significant new model of heaven emerged. The unexpected source was a distinguished Swedish intellectual and well-known experimental scientist, metallurgist and mathematician named Emanuel Swedenborg. In 1745, at the age of 56, Swedenborg had a vision which, according to one source "shook him, threw him to the ground and forced him to pray." Swedenborg himself wrote of an encounter with something "holy and indestructible."

His vision of the next world left him with clairvoyant powers and the ability to converse with angels. From his revelations, he constructed a model of heaven that included *everyone*: Christians, Jews, Buddhists, Moslems, saints and even sinners. In Swedenborg's heaven, each person would gravitate after death to communities of likeminded souls who had similar spiritual interests. "Like attracts like," he said, both in this and the next world. "To forestall any claim that this is an illusion or hallucination," he wrote in his book, *Heaven and Hell*, "I've been allowed to see them [angels] while I was fully awake, that is, my physical senses were in a state of clear perception."

Swedenborg's heaven was a busy place filled with worship, singing, learning and service. This displaced the image of a heaven where souls dwelled in a perpetual state of beatific worship and adoration before the Throne of God. He was the first to reveal that heaven was separated from Earth by only a thin veil through which we would pass immediately upon death, a concept still held by many Christians today.

Although God's presence is there, he said, we would not have direct contact with Him but would serve Him and love Him through "love and charity, shown to others in heaven."

Swedenborg was a pioneer, many years ahead of his time. It would be another 150 years before serious afterlife research would begin with the founding in the early 1880's of the English Society for Psychical Research. Data accumulated during the next 100 years not only confirmed many of Swedenborg's views of heaven, but expanded the

33

notion of heaven to encompass many higher levels of awareness. A picture has evolved since Swedenborg's time of a heaven where souls are mobile, so to speak, having the possibility of moving from the lowest levels, commonly referred to as hell, to countless higher realms and planes of consciousness.

SEVEN STAGES OF TRANSITION

It is now time to turn to what has come in direct communication to mediums from persons who have gone through transition, the completed experience of death, and are describing the other side as they experience it. To organize the information received through these channels, we will describe seven rather basic stages of transition. This will follow a model presented in the writings of a British scientist named Dr. Robert Crookall. In his 1961 book, *The Supreme Adventure*, he presents his comprehensive study of communications from persons who have gone through transition. They not only describe their dying experience but also their immediate afterlife. His book is a careful compilation of information, coming from over 100 sensitives (mediums) and some 150 books in publication. Surprisingly, from all these divergent sources, there still emerges a mass of compelling evidence that is quite coherent and consistent.

The stages of transition which are consistently described by Crookall's subjects and the other sources quoted in this book are as follows:

1.) The *call*: The dying seem to send out a call or signal to friends and relatives who have already gone to the other side. This call can be unconscious, but if there is a belief in survival, it is conscious and quite deliberate. Persons with whom there was a close personal link in life, usually relatives and friends, initially take the newly arrived dead into their care. This is certain to happen, according to most sources, if thoughts are sent out to them before death.

2.) The second stage is the *quick review of life*. When death is imminent and in fact has begun, the dying seem to have a quick review of their past life on Earth. It lasts for only a few minutes and should not be confused with the *judgement stage*, which comes later. "My entire life unveiled itself," one source said, "I clearly saw events of my life pass in a long procession before me. . . ."

3.) The third stage is the *shedding of the body from the soul*. The prelude to dying may involve suffering but the actual process of dying - disconnecting from the physical body - is absolutely painless and yet, it is a very critical phase in the whole process of transition. Indeed, some call it the most dramatic moment in life - the moment when the soul moves from one level of

35

consciousness to another. The dying process is one of the great sacred mysteries of the universe - simultaneously a death and a birth into a new reality in which we find ourselves completely healthy and whole. At the moment of leaving the body behind, one discarnate source said he was "dimly conscious of figures moving around the bed and I was floating in the air, a little above it. I saw the body stretched straight out. My first idea was that I might re-enter it, but soon all desire to do so left me. . . . The tie (silver cord) was broken."

4.) Stage four is the *sleep stage*. There seems to be more unanimity about a sleep stage following death than any of the other stages. The consensus is that the average person who dies a natural death sleeps between four and five days. The nature of that sleep varies with each individual, his or her age, the intensity of suffering prior to death and the spiritual evolvement of the individual. The sleep stage is a very necessary stage of conditioning before we enter the spirit world.

Those who have a deep-seated conviction that death is the absolute end have a very long sleep stage. Those, however, who expect to survive and have some knowledge of the next world do not necessarily need a sleep period unless they have had a long illness.

5.) The fifth stage is the *awakening*. One discarnate source said that the thing that impressed him most after a period of sleep was the intensified reality of everything. Everything was more brilliant, the trees, the flowers, the landscape. Again, there is repeated reference in these accounts to the fact that the degree of expanded consciousness immediately following death is in direct proportion to the degree of spiritual evolvement prior to death.

When souls slowly awaken from their sleep, they know where they are and who they are. Before the sleep stage, they are under the illusion that they are still in their physical bodies as they were on Earth. In most cases, this illusion is dispelled after the sleep period.

Some of the most descriptive material regarding the *awakening* stage is found in a book that was published in 1969 entitled *The Testimony of Light*, written by Helen Greaves, a little-known English sensitive who recorded communications from a woman named Frances Banks.

For fifteen years, Banks, an Anglican nun, was principal of a teacher's college in Grahamstown, South Africa. She was the author of two textbooks in psychology which were widely used. She and Helen Greaves were close friends. In the eight years prior to Frances Banks' death, she and Helen Greaves worked together in a prayer and meditation group. Helen Greaves describes in some detail what happened about three weeks after the time that Frances passed over. Sitting at home alone beside the fire, listening to music on the radio, she became aware of a presence. She switched off the radio and relaxed into a deep peace.

Slowly my whole being seemed to be caught up in a peace and beauty I cannot describe. I was conscious of being immersed in light. I was part of the light and yet the light issued from beyond me. I felt the nearness of spiritual presences. Somehow, I felt then that I was in touch with the soul of Frances Banks. The experience lasted about half an hour, then it gradually faded away.

Some days later the mind of Frances Banks began to impinge on the mind of Helen Greaves, who recorded the event. "I sat down, took my pen and began to write. Words, thoughts, sentences tumbled onto the paper. It is almost as though I took dictation. Yet this was not automatic writing. I was perfectly in control. I could feel that her mind was using mine. . . ." She knew then that the discarnate mind of Frances Banks and her incarnate mind had linked together in telepathic communication. She felt strongly that she was to be the channel for something Frances had to say. Here is how Frances Banks described her awakening to Helen Greaves.

A minute after you die you will be exactly the same! . . . as soon as I was able to bring myself to a conscious state of mind, I knew that I was the same in essence. True, I felt light, and there was a sense of freedom that was bewildering. . . . One of my first recollections was, "I am still conscious." The change has taken place. . . .

And for a time I seemed to lose my identity. . . .
I recall endeavoring anxiously to pierce through
this new state to recall memory. . . . At length I
recall telling myself to go to sleep, and in a way
that is what I must have done. . . .

But the next time I came back to consciousness I seemed to be pulling myself up out of
a thin sea of silver. . . . Those are the only words
I can use to describe the experience. . . . And the
first face I saw was the smiling one of my dear
Mother in religion, Mother Florence. . . . But now
I found I was lying in an open porch with a vista
of blue and silver before me. This was beautiful
beyond words and calming to my spirit. Trouble,
anxiety and all sense of loss abated; a great
feeling of peace enwrapped me. . . .

'This is it,' I kept assuring myself in wonder. 'I have made the change.'

6.) The sixth stage is the *judgment*. The idea of a final
judgment after death has a long tradition, but there
seems to be more confusion about this stage than about
any other stage of transition. The popular concept of
The Judgment is that some Great Being will arbitrarily
separate the sheep from the goats, the saints from the
sinners, and decide who may or who may not enter
heaven. The consensus of these psychic sources, however, is that the *judgment* is not a single, isolated, one-
time event but rather an extended period of self-evalua-
tion by our own conscience, our higher self. It is a

process in which we are helped to recognize our failures and successes, our shortcomings and our inner strengths. The judgment referred to here can only come when a soul is prepared and willing to face up to itself.

During the *judgment*, we become aware for the first time of the little things of which we were previously unaware on Earth: sins of omission, sins of selfishness, intolerance, indifference, arrogance and greed. It is a time when the dictum "know thyself" takes on a new dimension; a time when truth is made clear and the soul can evaluate its own successes and failures, its strengths and weaknesses.

Dr. Raynor Johnson, one of the great minds in this field, said, "All judgment is self-judgment. There is a center of the soul of every man. This is the divine spark and this is what judges him."

The *judgment* period does not always begin as soon as we arrive on the other side. Some take a long time to face the ordeal, at which time each soul will undergo its unique judgment experience.

In the case of Frances Banks, two "blueprints" were brought together in her consciousness.

One is the Perfect Idea with which my spirit went bravely into incarnation. The other is my life as it was actually lived. . . . This is the first shock; a true humbling of yourself to find you did so little when you would have done so much; that you went wrong so often when you were sure you were right.

During this experience, the whole cycle of your life unfolds before you. . . . During this crisis one seems to be entirely alone. Yours is the judgment. You stand at your own bar of judgment. You make your own decisions. You take your own blame. . . . You are the accused, the judge and the jury.

Banks speaks of a second stage that began when she felt strong enough to face her Earth life, chapter by chapter. During this time, however, she never felt alone. She felt "someone" beside her at all times.

My own High Spirit or a Great Helper, I have yet to discover. You must judge what you did and why and what were the results [good or bad] . . . , this Great Being beside you giving you strength, peace and tranquility and helping with constructive criticism. This is a wonderful experience, though harrowing at times. But very cleansing and bringing new hope.

The Swiss researcher, Albert Pauchard, in communication with his sister soon after his death in 1935, spoke of a judgment that, "removes all of the comfortable padding which people use to justify their actions and hide their real motives. . . ."

Every one of us, no matter who he may be, has at the bottom of his being a layer of dregs, of

41

which he is not aware. I did not know how true that was until I came here.

We are good people, you and I, and when coming here I expected to find only glory and delight, but after the first feeling of liberation has passed, we are brought . . . directly face to face with the various departments of our "I."

I assure you that it is then, and only then, that one learns what self-knowledge means. . . . You cannot even imagine all the revelations that result from our objective encounters with our "I" when seen under . . . different aspects. There are some very unpleasant moments to pass through, I can assure you.

In a conversation with his sister, some twelve months after his death, he related a judgment experience, reported to him by someone he met on the other side. This new friend told him that at one point he had had to pass through a dense fog in which he saw the moving figure of a man he recognized as someone he thoroughly disliked. He looked away only to find that the image still persisted. Even when he closed his eyes he could see the figure. Presently, the image changed and he recognized another man he disliked. This was repeated over and over again.

People who once horrified him appeared and disappeared in succession before him. It was a kind of trial disagreeable beyond expression.

Finally, after he was completely exhausted, he appealed to his guide for help.

At once he heard a fatherly voice saying, "but look well my child! Stop projecting your own image upon another and condemning him. . . . Look who those specters are."

Then to his great horror, he recognized himself in all of these forms [and said], "They had been created by my own attitudes toward the people I had spoken of."

Paul Beard wrote that judgment is an ongoing process, a process of self-knowledge at the deepest levels.

It's purpose is not punishment, but education. It is non-vengeful and beneficent in its effect . . . it is the Divine Will expressing itself with infinite justice, patience and love towards one of the beings this Will has created, to help him to overcome all that is fallible in him.

The process is not one of weighing of our good deeds against our bad deeds. All shortcomings of our life, regardless of how much good we have done on Earth, must be overcome and the spiritual disabilities corrected. This will require persistence and much hard work, sometimes mental suffering, pain, sorrow and many lifetimes.

7.) The seventh stage is called the *post-judgment* or the *assignment stage*. It is interesting to note in the case of Frances Banks that three months after she passed over, according to the dated script, she was assigned to a team whose job it was to receive souls from Earth and other worlds. She says many times that the soul always graduates to its rightful place, the place it has earned and prepared for itself.

She temporarily lived in a community that helped "souls to awaken to greater freedom before they proceed onward to their rightful places." Perhaps because Banks was a spiritually advanced soul, due to her lifelong work as a spiritual counselor and teacher on Earth, she began, three months after her death, to serve with a group of others, to help arriving souls from Earth. She said, "Our work is to be on hand when those newly arrived awaken to their new environment. Sometimes friends and relatives are there to greet them and we wait in the background until the greetings are over."

Given the number of persons who go through physical death every day, it is little wonder that many discarnate sources report that they are assigned tasks related to helping to orient "newcomers" in heaven. The *assignment stage* has a definite rhyme and reason in the context of the development and inclinations of the individual soul. In the following chapters, we will hear more about the various activities engaged in by those who have communicated about their experiences.

Chapter Three

Post-Transition life

"Now you just remember this heaven is as blissful and lovely as it can be; but it's just the busiest place you ever heard of. There ain't any idle people here after the first day. Singing hymns and waving palm branches through all eternity is pretty when you hear about it in the pulpit but it's as poor way to put in valuable time as a body could contrive. . . . Eternal Rest sounds comforting in the pulpit, too. Well, you can try it once and see how heavy time will hang on your hands. . . .

"Why, Stonefield, a man like you, that had been active and stirring all his life, would go mad in six months in a heaven where he hadn't anything to do. Heaven is the very last place to come to rest in and don't you be afraid to bet on that!"

Mark Twain, *Captain Stonefield's First Visit to Heaven*

HEAVEN, according to all sources, is indeed a busy place filled with exciting activities and endless opportunities. Certainly there will be times of worship for those who wish to worship, time to play and pray and meditate. What we do, in large measure, depends upon our soul's interests and our level of spiritual evolvement prior to death.

The vast majority will expect a carefree, painfree, pleasure-filled paradise, a kind of "super-welfare state" where they will dream away eternity. Many will do what they have always done on Earth, enjoy a comfortable, happy life in a community of like-minded people. Some will garden, some will play games, build houses and generally socialize with others in their community. Those who are spiritually more advanced will participate in some form of service, helping the spiritually retarded, the troubled children, the suicides and those confused and frightened souls who died suddenly in wars, earthquakes, floods, famines, plagues and other catastrophic events.

The next world will provide each soul with countless opportunities to grow and become more aware of the "many mansions" of consciousness beyond the Earth plane. Endless opportunities to learn and advance are available for those who are curious and interested. "I'm learning to understand the beauty of words and rhythms of music in a painting," one discarnate source said, "all are a part of the soul's development." In the next world, we can study in libraries, attend lectures and visit other centers of learning. According to the discarnate Lutheran Minister, A. D. Mattson, "Art galleries, museums in the astral world contain replicas of the great art of the ages. . . ." Another source said she was now able to really paint what she wants to. "You know, I've never really been satisfied with anything I did - I feel now that at last I'm beginning to paint as the real me."

The quest for wisdom certainly does not end with physical death. In Plato's *Apology*, Socrates said, after he was condemned to die, "I shall continue my search into true and false knowledge: as in this world, also in that. I shall find out who is wise, who pretends to be wise and who is not . . . what infinite delight would there be in conversing with the wise and asking them questions."

After an initial period of exhilaration, experiencing the wonder and awe of the new world, a world free of pain, many will settle back into a life of spiritual laziness, enjoying a life of ease on some comfortable astral plane. For others, according to Maurice Barbanell, who after his death communicated with Paul Beard, this ecstasy is replaced by a sense of urgency to know more, "almost a hunger for more." He warns that the most difficult task in the next world, as it is on Earth, is fighting spiritual lassitude. Beard wrote of this in *Light Magazine*.

It is a common idea that once we have passed through death, reality at every level can become revealed without any change in your own level of consciousness. Nothing could be further from the truth. The higher the spiritual ladder is climbed, the more the effort to climb further is intensified because more is demanded of the climber. Serious guides and [spiritual] teachers speak of the hard work to be faced both here and in the next world, the need to work on one's soul.

It appears that Captain Stonefield's vision about the active life in heaven was accurate, and, as we will see, the activity is ultimately oriented around service and the refinement of the soul.

47

A WORLD OF ACTIVITY

Sally Lehmann, the daughter of the English author and
editor, Rosamond Lehmann, in one of her many messages
to her mother, speaks of helping spiritually retarded souls
on the lower level into which she carries the Light.

It is rather an exciting job because the
more one does the better the results become. I
think magnetically many are drawn to the Light
in spite of themselves. . . . I have a family and I
go about with them, they come from a dark slum
and with care they are growing delightfully.

Sally Lehmann was once asked if she ever saw angels.

We see them from time to time and they
mingle closely with [highly] evolved spirits like
the saints. . . . The first time I saw an angel I
was entranced. There was this marvelous irides-
cent body - no wings, I think, as we used to paint
them - but flaming with color far more vibrant
than any of us; they cast us into shadows. I
looked and looked at this angel and I asked why
she, (I think it was a she!) was there. She was
standing quite still, and I was told that she was
sending rays into newly-built churches, mosques
and temples on earth. . . .

After the newly arrived have adapted themselves to the new life, some have the urge to travel, to explore, to widen their horizons of the universe. Ambrose Pratt, Australian journalist and naturalist, in a communication to Raynor Johnson, reported an exciting traveling experience. He was free, he said, "to choose a guide for the adventure." Since he was a contemporary and great admirer of George W. Russell, an Irish mystic and poet, he asked him to be his "philosopher-guide."

> Once you know how to travel, you need only to think where you wish to go and you will be there or you can take the same journey as leisurely as you would on Earth. We traversed the Sahara Desert, we visited the poles, we absorbed the human life of great cities. We visited the lonely Himalayas, the Rockies. We went East, West and South and North perceiving the outer and then experiencing the inner sections. . . . I visited the country of Tibet's sacred center . . . the dream-land of Iona. I rode upon the winds, rode over the waves, leaped the mountains.

As on Earth, religious groups in heaven will continue to worship according to their traditions for as long as they wish. Mattson indicated that sects and religious people tend to meet in small groups and have their meetings in what they feel is their heaven.

I am told by my teacher, that eventually they become bored with their narrowness and their own helpers and teachers try to give them another thought, another idea, to help them see and break away from their narrow approach . . . you need never change unless you wish. God gives us perfect freedom in the spirit. . . .

After a time, these souls suddenly have a tremendous experience knowing that all love is one, under God, and there is no division in purpose.

BORDERLAND

In *The Silent Road,* Tudor Pole wrote that some souls are totally dedicated to helping anywhere there is suffering and distress. One such volunteer gave an account of his experiences.

There [exists] a borderline region, where [there are] a number of groups and organizations similar in function to our Red Cross Society on earth. Their numbers are drawn from those who have been specially trained. . . . I spent much of my time in the company of suicides, influencing them, helping them to break out of their darkness. It is for me as dangerous as nursing in a hospital of contagious diseases in your world, but I chose the job of my own free will. . . .

When we realize that approximately half a million souls arrive from the planet Earth each day, at every level of the astral world, we recognize the endless opportunities for service. Many of these are children. One source, a man who worked with confused adults, said there was an especially large influx of children from areas of the world where there is widespread starvation and suffering. Another reported that he worked "among terrified children who died before their time through the war (WW II). They cry for their mothers and cannot find them. Often their souls are injured and they are utterly helpless and pitiful."

Edgar Cayce, Frederic Myers and others spoke of a period of two or three terrestrial days spent in what they called a "borderland," an intermediate state through which we pass between Earth and the astral planes. This stage is referred to in some literature as hades. It is not, however, the hades of "hell-fire and damnation," but rather a stage of adjustment, a time of changing from physical vibration to a higher spiritual vibration.

Myers, speaking through Geraldine Cummins, described his experience of the "borderland."

I died in Italy. I was very weary at the time of my passing. For me, hades was a place of rest, a place of half lights and drowsy peace. As a man regains his strength after a long sleep so did I gather spiritual and intellectual force needed during the time I abode in hades.

Cayce had a recurring dream while giving life readings over a period of several years. In it he found himself moving in consciousness through ascending astral levels where he encountered different forms and different conditions from the lowest "shadowland" to a world of beauty and light. The misshapen forms he saw were externalized deep-seated emotions: hate, fear and passions of every form.

I knew my spirit, mind and soul were separated from my body and that I was seeking information for another. I passed the outer darkness so dark that it actually hurt, yet there was a stream of light that I knew I must follow and nothing on either side of the light must detract from my purpose. . . .

As I passed along the line of light, I became conscious of forms, of movement crowding toward the light. Coming to the next plane . . ., I realized that the forms of movement or figures were taking shape not as humans, but rather the exaggeration of human desire. Passing on a little further, these forms were gradually lost; still I had the consciousness that they were seeking the light—or more light. Then the figures gradually took form, continually coming toward the light.

Finally, I passed through a place where individuals appeared just as they are today - men and women - but satisfied with their position. The number of individuals in this state of satisfaction continued to grow, and then there were homes and cities where they were content to continue as they were.

Still following the light, which grew stronger and stronger, I heard music in the beyond. Then there came a space where all was springtime, all was a-blossom, all was summer. Some were happy, some desired to remain but many were pressing on and on to the place where there might be greater understanding, more light, more to be gained. Then I reached a place where I was seeking the records of the lives of people who had lived in the earth.[1]

Many souls come to the other side, Frances Banks said, who have lived evil lives on Earth. In their remorse and shame, they isolate themselves by going to the lower regions of the astral world and join other such souls who need help and guidance before they can join those in the higher levels.

The lower regions are described as places of gloom and dark emotions. The notion of hell as a place of eternal suffering is never mentioned by discarnate sources; they speak only of a "shadowland" populated with murderers, rapists, terrorists, the chronically evil. These are hells of the mind, dark states of misery, of hate and passions carried over from their Earth life. They can always choose

---

[1]From *The Continuity of Life*, the transcription of a lecture by Edgar Cayce, copyright by A.R.E., 1958. Used with permission.

to change, to ask for help from souls of higher levels who will help them follow the spiritual path of love and harmony. According to Paul Beard, it is no light matter to enter these realms with the intention to help.

> To enter these areas fills rescuers with a deep sense of distress; these helpers, sensitive men and women, can themselves become affected and drawn into some of the purblind emotions they seek to lift from others. And if they remain too long in this area they declare they can, to some extent, become temporarily overcome by them. . . . Evil is powerful at its own level and clearly a rescuer needs sterner qualities than those of the self-congratulatory do-gooder. . . ."

THE EDUCATION OF THE SOUL

According to these discarnate sources, suffering on these planes will not completely cease. Certainly there will be periods of great joy, peace and fulfillment, as well as periods of sorrow and deep concern for those still on Earth who may be suffering from disease, wars or other catastrophic events. As long as there are lessons to be learned, attitudes to be changed, there will surely be periods when we will experience suffering, regrets, and sometimes frustrations and discouragement as part of our spiritual development.

Whoever we are, we do not suddenly become saints or omniscient spirits when we die. We survive with all our memories intact, our accumulated wisdom and talents, our attitudes, prejudices and beliefs. Spiritually, morally and intellectually, we arrive in the next world exactly as we left the Earth, no better, no worse.

In this new, light-filled world, our astral bodies will be just as solid and real to us as our physical bodies appeared to be on Earth. Although we will be liberated from the body, we will not be free of matter. In other realms of consciousness, matter is more subtle, and it is felt at least as acutely as it is in the physical body.

This next world is a subtler plane of faster vibrations responsive to our thoughts and wishes. Here the houses, trees, rivers and flowers will seem every bit as solid to us because they will be vibrating on the same frequency as our new bodies. This is easier to understand when we know that solid matter here on Earth appears hard to us but is actually composed of widely spaced, vibrating atoms of energy. Frances Banks reported that her astral body was made of a finer composition than the physical body. "Here I look as I did on earth, but I am free to refashion my body by thought."

The average person who suffers a long, painful, terminal illness on Earth will be surprised to find himself or herself with a new astral body, whole and pain-free. If in previous incarnations we have developed a capacity to love, to be tolerant, compassionate and unselfish, we will automatically gravitate to higher levels of consciousness and greater awareness which opens doors to ever greater opportunities for service, growth and development.

Those, however, who were spiritually depraved, devoid of love, without pity and compassion will quickly find themselves in the lower astral planes in a dismal, dark world with others of similar nature. Others who are in a less spiritually degenerated state, but whose characters are deeply flawed with coarseness, bigotry, intolerance and self-centeredness will have bodies which others will perceive as diseased. All of these require help and nurture from dedicated spiritual counselors from higher planes before they can join the mainstream of life in the new world. They will discover that when they think negative thoughts and feel negative emotions, these will externalize and take on appearances of their own. They must either learn to discipline their thoughts and feelings in order to avoid embarrassing situations in their relationships with others or move to lower levels of the astral plane to join other immature, adolescent souls.

Suffering in the next world will be unlike suffering on Earth where we sometimes experience unexpected misfortune and tragedies for no apparent reason. In the spirit world, sorrows are very real, but the *cause* of sorrows and suffering will be clearly understood as part of the growth process.

Souls cannot be helped, however, against their will because free will is just as inviolate on the astral planes as it is here. When suffering has done its remedial work, they will ask for help which is always readily available.

Chapter Four

New Clay to Mold

IN THE NEXT WORLD, our powers of imagination are greatly expanded, and we will live more directly with what we imagine than we do on Earth. For imagination is the spontaneous spark of the Great Creative Mind living in each of us. The more we develop our awareness, the greater our creative powers become. But we cannot change the whole scene around us because it does not belong to us alone; the many beings with whom we share the surroundings influence the environment with their imaginations as well. We create only within certain limits, as long as we do not disturb the welfare and happiness of those around us. Frederic Myers described the situation from his level of awareness.

> You can control, form, and draw life to it just as a sculptor forms and shapes clay. You do not create your surroundings through your own conscious acts or thoughts. Your emotional desires and your deeper mind manufacture these without your being actually aware of the process.

Of course, food is not necessary because the astral body absorbs its energy from the cosmic rays of its environment. Usually there are set times or cycles for recharging our new body. "Such periods," Myers said, "have some analogy to sleep during which time the soul withdraws from all contacts with other souls. While in this passive, withdrawn state, the soul reaches up to its Spirit and its mind renews itself."

Because food is not necessary, we do not spend our time and energy earning a livelihood as we do on Earth. This leaves us more time to explore the limitless beauties of the universe. Spiritually serious souls, said Paul Beard, will be working not to earn money but working to grow in consciousness.

Our natural tendency is to appear just as we did on Earth. In the early stages after physical death, the creation of clothes comes to us unconsciously from the depths of the imaginative mind. Once we recognize our creative powers, however, we can create for ourselves clothes that suit our tastes and personality.

Earth marriages will prevail on the astral planes if the relationship has been truly loving and sincere. If one partner finds himself or herself on one of the lower levels, the more advanced soul can always go to the spouse for brief visits to encourage and teach the spiritually less mature partner. If, however, one of the partners is unwilling to grow, the couple will eventually drift apart.

The family unit stays together only if all are willing to develop spiritually and increase in the capacity to serve the needs of others. Those members of the family who initially gravitate to the lower levels can occasionally go up to the higher planes, but for only short periods because they cannot tolerate the higher vibrational fields there. Members of a family who are already living on the other side sometimes linger in a kind of holding pattern while they wait for other members still on Earth to join them before they proceed on to higher planes. It can also happen that one member leaves the family in order to live on higher planes.

In one of her messages to Helen Greaves, Frances Banks tells of an experience which she had when she accompanied an advanced guide to higher levels and saw a new aspect of life on higher planes.

> Neither of us could hold this great intensity of vibration for long. We felt (so to speak) used up by this High Frequency so that presently, I for one, had the strange experience of dwindling and then we were both back in my garden. . . .

Albert Pauchard was possibly speaking of the same phenomenon.

> In a world such as I am living in at present all animosity, selfishness, distrust or exclusiveness of any kind are impossible. Anything that even slightly resembles such is automatically excluded. Only such things which are in unison with the vibrations of a plane, can reach that plane and exist on it.

An open mind is of the utmost importance when we arrive in the next world. In one of his communications, Pauchard gave an example of this in the case of a man and his twin sister. They both belonged to a very orthodox Christian sect. The brother, a priest, was a very pious, honest but intolerant person, imprisoned in his own dogma. He seemed to fear God more than he loved Him. Pauchard said this man "lived in a joyless, colorless world as he had done on earth" and that his sermons were still "threatening and lifeless."

His sister, on the other hand, belonged to the same sect and while she shared his belief in the same creeds, she was not imprisoned by them. "Her soul soared beyond the limits of the faith she professed. She was a woman with a great heart and universal sympathies."

Both were equally virtuous, equally conscientious and faithful, and yet for one, doctrine prevented the expansion of the spirit. For the other, the same doctrine was a cocoon in which a caterpillar could transform itself into a butterfly.

Those who expect to see God face to face in the next world will probably be disappointed. God, of course, is fully present there just as He is on this plane. But there, as here, we contact Him by prayer and meditation. No one, of course, can determine to whom Christ may appear, and none of the many persons who have communicated from this level of the astral plane ever speaks of having seen Christ. All, however, say that the more they expand their consciousness, the more sensitive they become to the Divine Presence. It seems improbable that God would limit Himself to an astral body, but God and the Christ are an all-pervading presence that can be felt by everyone.

To look upon these Divine Presences with all of their brilliance and high vibrations would be disastrous. Raynor Johnson draws a fine analogy by saying that we "can have a real awareness of the unclouded radiance of the sun as they go about their daily paths, but they seek to gaze into the sun at their own peril."

There is a general agreement among these sources that we can find ourselves after physical death in challenging, creative interaction with our heavenly surroundings. Much more than on Earth, we will confront what we most deeply believe. While heaven will be colored by our belief about what heaven should be, we will also be guided by our soul's longing for a greater life of love and service. This longing comes from our true depths and, even in heaven, will provide us with new horizons.

Chapter Five

The Many Planes of Heaven

A SECOND DEATH AND REBIRTH

MANY WILL REMAIN in the first heaven for many years, sometimes centuries, content with their condition, with no further aspirations or thought of further growth. They are the men and women who fear change and do not have the spiritual urge to grow beyond their familiar, comfortable astral homes. They are reluctant to take the next uncertain step in the soul's journey to higher heavens. These well-meaning, but unquestioning people envision heaven as the final resting place, a place free of struggle and stress, free of suffering and pain.

After a time, however, varying with each individual, a few souls will become slowly aware of an inner stirring, an intuitive knowing that, even here, life is incomplete. They sense that there are higher levels to reach, more to learn and achieve. They begin to feel a spiritual discontent and a sense of unfulfillment.

These searching souls begin to recognize that much of their first heaven was created out of their own self-fulfilling desires. They are not sufficiently challenged now, nor are their pleasures spiritually rewarding. They realize they are still far from reaching their spiritual potential, and are convinced that there is still a long, unexplored journey ahead of them, a greater part of life still to come. Myers depicted this in his communications.

> There is an eternal law, which compels the seeker after Beauty and Truth to endeavour with all his might to reach the plane from which, mounting still higher, he may draw near to God. Always the soul has the power to choose, and if the individual is deficient in imaginative power and in faith, he will have no desire to go forward.

Some, out of choice, remain in these astral planes to wait for other family members and loved ones so together they can move to the next higher levels of awareness to a new stage of enlightenment. Several years after his death, Ambrose Pratt communicated on this subject to Raynor Johnson.

> . . . a few of my Group-soul and fewer still of those dear and intimate mortals who were in the design of my past earthly life are still living in the physical body. I must be there to greet them and aid them in their development after their demise. So my routine life at present is passed within the radius of the earth. . . .

He explained, however, that by the time Johnson passed over, he, Pratt, may be living temporarily at an even more advanced state and would not be able to greet him. He went on to say, however, that if Johnson would send out a mental call after death, he would appear in his earthly likeness so that Johnson would recognize him.

Once the decision is made to advance beyond the astral planes, each soul will experience a *second death,* at which the soul is born into a new life in a new heaven on what is called by some sources "the fourth plane." This second death, however, comes only when a soul is spiritually prepared and willing to take the next important step in its spiritual journey. A discarnate described his second death to Paul Beard.

> It is not separation [but] a feeling of complete serenity and peace, with no concern for anything, or awareness of people around you . . . you are supported by something that is almost unidentifiable, you have lost your own identity without any concern or anxiety about it. . . . It is a true spiritual release, and for a little while you don't really know where you are . . . there is no feeling of distress. It is a kind of oblivion, but a conscious oblivion. . . .
>
> Then you become aware . . . of what I can only describe as a harmonic reverberation around you, a beautiful ecstasy. . . . You feel this divine ecstatic, unified power with such indescribable joy that you just don't know what is happening to you. . . .

Others who describe this state speak of a calming of all processes, a great stillness. Arthur Conan Doyle, author of the Sherlock Holmes detective stories, speaking through the medium Grace Cooke, described this transition as the shedding of the astral body when the soul enters higher planes. According to Doyle, "after passing through what are known as astral planes, we shed a shell, 'the dress' or 'envelope' which housed the soul in its astral life."

About this step in transition, Edgar Cayce said regarding astral bodies which have been discarded that "some - those that appear as images - are the expressions or shells or [astral] bodies of an individual which has been left [behind] when its soul self has projected on[ward] and [which] has not yet been dissolved. . . ."[2]

This is a time of a rebirth in which new vistas open for us. We discover that we possess a great untapped potential of which we were not previously aware. We gain a greater understanding of the universe and a new, enlarged consciousness.

A WORLD OF IDEAS AND FEELINGS

The fourth plane is often called a world of artists, a realm in which music and form find their perfection. On this plane, as well as on the astral planes, however, we still learn through suffering, struggle and work. Only through suffering can we purge our egos' wants and desires and prepare ourselves for even higher worlds, higher heavens.

Sorrow and ecstasy are known, but they are not of the variety that we know on Earth. Sorrow and ecstasy

---

[2]From Edgar Cayce Reading 516-4, A.R.E. Used with permission.

both have a spiritual dimension which is not recognized on the material plane. As on other planes, there are sub-levels of awareness, and the rate of vibration and intensity of light increases as the soul moves up the ladder of consciousness. With each new level, we experience an awareness of new realities.

We should not look at these different levels as sharp divisions but rather as a range of interpenetrating levels of consciousness. The higher the levels of awareness the greater our spiritual and intellectual understanding. Here, too, we will find ourselves among a high order of souls and celestial beings with whom we share experiences, work together on divine missions and help other aspiring souls to reach these same planes of understanding.

We break away from our ego-centered personality traits and patterns and realize, as never before, that we, indeed, have a greater higher self of which our earthly personality is only one aspect, one facet of our total self. On this level all racial, religious and philosophical barriers cease to exist. We begin to sense universal truths that encompass the basic aspects of all religions.

Here we make contact with the source of all higher inspirations. "You find ultimate beauty and form," Raynor Johnson said, "where the dreams of artists and sculptors and visionaries are realized." It is on this plane that the archetypes of great music, poetry and art exist. Myers called this a world of colors, lights and music, our appearance "a compound of light and color unimaginable."

From this level, earthly musicians, in peak moments of inspiration, capture complete symphonies from the mind of a master musician. French musician Caesar Franck

67

seemed to be describing such a moment when he said he heard a piece of music "playing" in his mind, knew it was already composed, complete and perfect and his task was simply to write it down.

From this plane of universal consciousness and attunement to God, highly evolved souls, as members of a Divine Society, are designated "governors or rulers" of all the life processes and affairs of Earth or of planets in other solar systems and even other stars. Myers referred to these highly enlightened beings as "The Wise" who control processes of nature, the duration of life and the intricate patterns of karma. They are agents, surrogates of God, whose "work proceeds downward to the smallest detail."

They are not capable, however, of changing or adding to the Supreme Idea, but they are empowered by God to help sustain, guide and carry out His law in the cosmos. To some, this may sound blasphemous, but they forget that we, too, are divine beings, created in the image and likeness of God and, as such, co-creators. God's ultimate purpose for our immortal souls is that we become celestial, angelic beings who also play important roles in the vast scheme of the cosmos.

Man's ultimate purpose and destination is not to spend eternity in a pleasure-filled paradise perpetually worshiping God but to attain to ever-higher levels of consciousness through endless evolutionary stages of development. During many lifetimes on Earth and jour-neys through many worlds and spheres, we can eventually reach the spiritual status of a Great Being and participate in the infinite processes of the universe.

Jesus was clearly speaking of man's great potential when he said, "He that believeth on me, the works that I do shall he do also; and greater works than these shall he do" (John 14:12). We forget that we are all "gods-in-the-making," divinely fashioned, immortal souls with limitless potential and vast, unfilled powers. We never, however, lose our individuality, our true self, even as part of the imagination of God. It is no wonder that Paul having glimpsed into the Third Heaven said that God was preparing for us an "eternal weight of glory far beyond all comparison" (2 Cor. 4:17).

69

Chapter Six

Reincarnation

WHY WE COME BACK

OUR SOUL'S JOURNEY through many lifetimes is governed by the principles of *karma*, the law of cause and effect, and *reincarnation*, the soul's opportunity to return to Earth to learn certain lessons that can only be learned here. For the spiritually immature soul, rebirth is inevitable. Its purpose is to give us as many lifetimes on Earth as necessary to gain the spiritual growth needed to make further rebirths unnecessary. It is an integral part of our soul's long process of development.

Joseph Leeming, in *Yoga and the Bible,* gives a simple analogy that explains how the twin principles of karma and reincarnation make each of us responsible for our future joys and sorrows.

Each day is like a furrow lying before us, our thoughts, desires and actions are the seeds that each moment we drop into it even though we do not perceive what seeds we are planting. When the furrow is completed we commence another. Each day represents a fresh one and so on to the end of life, sowing and ever sowing, and all we have sown springs up, grows, bears fruit, either in this life or a succeeding one.

It is the Christian equivalent, in the context of many lifetimes, of "Whatsoever a man soweth, that shall he also reap." (Gal. 6:7) and, "With what measure ye mete, it shall be measured to you" (Mark 4:24).

When we see injustices, tragedies, personal entanglements, sickness and suffering of the apparently innocent, these are reflections on the physical level of serious indiscretions in some past lifetime. The recognition of our soul's pre-existence comes to some suddenly as a glorious epiphany that gives inner conviction of this great truth. The process of reincarnation itself, however, has always been a mystery.

Kathleen Raine, English poet and author, in a series of essays on George Russell, the Irish poet and mystic, in *Light,* 1975, reported a conversation which the English author, Constance Sitwell, had with him. "He remembered glimpses," she said, of "brief but very vivid Druidic times in Ireland; of a Spanish life, riding into a walled town and fighting: one Egyptian period, and a very far back life in India. . . ." He told her of these and other recollections of his own previous incarnations, memories which aided him in his growth because they gave him assurances of the immortality of his soul.

In her book *Many Mansions,* Dr. Gina Cerminara refers to many of Edgar Cayce's life readings which provide strong evidence of previous lives and the operation of the law of cause and effect. Hundreds of people came to him with every thinkable kind of physical infirmity. Many were told that their problems resulted from some physical or mental cruelty they had imposed on others in a past life. A college professor, who was born blind, was told that in a Persian incarnation he had deliberately blinded a prisoner of war. A man who suffered from digestive problems which were not only uncomfortable but also embarrassing was told that in two successive incarnations he had been an incorrigible glutton. Yet another man who suffered from deafness was informed that he had ignored pleas for help when he was in a position to help. Many of Cayce's readings referred to by Cerminara pointed out that some afflictions resulted from mocking and jeering the Christians who were publicly mutilated in a Roman arena. Others were told that their handicaps came from some past arrogance and selfishness.

In a striking example of good karma, a young woman was told that her present physical beauty came from faithfully performing menial tasks in a convent with a spirit of acceptance and love in a previous life.

Without the notion of reincarnation, it is difficult to explain the wide spiritual and moral differences between people, some near-saints, inherently good, others morally and spiritually depraved. It seems virtually impossible that these tremendous disparities could have developed in a single lifetime. Without an understanding of reincarnation, we look in vain for hidden answers to life's most difficult problems.

Reincarnation and the law of karma also help explain why there are persons burdened with the care of spouses who may be dying from a slow, disabling illness or parents who spend years, sometimes an entire lifetime, caring for a retarded child. These great principles are the rhyme and reason behind the fact that some children are born with healthy bodies and minds to devoted parents in an environment of opportunity and happiness while others are born crippled, blind, mentally retarded, abused or in impoverished circumstances. When we realize that every newly-born child comes into the world as a soul with a past history, then we can understand the seeming injustices. We know then that all of our joys, our successes, failures, sorrows and pain are the consequences of our own past life choices.

This also explains some aspects of genius. Those who diligently hone their special inherent talents lifetime after lifetime will, in subsequent incarnations, become brilliant performers in their chosen discipline, whether it be music, art, the sciences or mathematics. Those who, early in their lives, feel strong compulsive urges to pursue a certain vocation are simply following innate skills developed in past lives.

Musical prodigies like Chopin, Mozart, Beethoven and others could, at a very early age, compose and execute musical compositions with knowledge and skill far beyond their chronological age. It strongly suggests that a child prodigy is the incarnation of a soul with a very specialized previous development. Plato believed that any skill easily mastered comes from skills carried over from past lives.

It explains the sometimes striking contrast in talents, personality traits, temperament and sensitivity, even among children of the same parents, reared in the same home environment. Each child reflects or exhibits his or her own dominant past life traits, skills and behavior patterns. During its many incarnations, the soul records all experiences, retains memories of skills and gathered wisdom from those past lives, some of which may exhibit themselves in the current lifetime.

We incarnate with those whom we have hated or loved, helped or hindered so that we can undo karmic bonds and pay back karmic debts that have tied us to those persons in the past. Instances are cited of presently incarnated souls, who have come back into Earth in order to work out unresolved relationships with roots reaching back as far as ancient Egypt. Paul Beard speaks of reincarnation and karma as opportunities.

> [We tend] to look upon karma as a bad debt we must repay in terms of unhappiness . . . [but] it is equally important not to overlook other happier, though unglamorous threads: the purpose of events and meetings is not only to redress, but it is also to enhance, to take forward what has been commenced in earlier days. . . . Thus one meets persons who have a particular[ly] beneficent influence upon one: some seem to put tools in one's hands which have been lacking before; others open doors of opportunities . . . and help to develop, perhaps out of a love relationship, new talents and gifts or more shapely characteristics.

The one great lesson that becomes clearly evident in this picture of reincarnation is that each of us has responsibility for our own condition in life. There is no one to blame - not God, not others, not bad luck or fate. Always, we are confronted by our own past and we are likewise always fashioning our own future.

The long process of spiritual evolution comes through suffering and sorrow, through love, compassion and service to others, but never without purpose, justice or mercy. Suffering is sometimes the only way to force some reluctant souls into greater spiritual awareness. Sometimes we are forced to live with prolonged illness and sorrow, with moments of desperation that makes us feel a dependence upon a power outside ourselves. This opens centers within our souls that reveal to us our soul's deepest need, the need to change our way of life. "Through suffering," White Eagle told Grace Cooke, "man's spirit is awakened and the long adventure of his return to heaven begins."

On Earth, on the astral planes and other higher levels, a great cosmic drama unfolds constantly, as millions of souls go through births and deaths in ever-ascending cycles of spiritual development and growth. Some lose, some gain in a single lifetime but each soul is proceeding and experiencing according to its own particular needs and requirements.

TIME BETWEEN LIVES

The amount of time that elapses between incarnations is the subject of much speculation. The Hindus and Tibetans believe that the frequency of incarnation is determined by the spiritual maturity of the soul in its last life. The more mature the soul, the more time elapses between incarnations.

According to Gautama Buddha, physical bodies are hard to come by. Incarnation is, therefore, sometimes delayed until a suitable body is born into the Earth at the right time and in the right place so as to provide the soul the appropriate family and social environment in which it can learn lessons necessary to further spiritual growth. One Himalayan tradition charts history in cycles of approximately 6000 years. According to this tradition, we are presently approaching the end of one such period. There is always a surge of souls seeking incarnation at the end of these great cycles, and this may account for the dramatic increase in world population in the modern era.

There is no fixed law, Myers said, which determines the time between the soul's earthly incarnations.

[At a certain point in the soul's progress,] the soul reflects, weighs and considers the facts of his own nature . . . the spirit helps you choose your future. You have complete free will, but your spirit indicates the path you should follow.

I can assure you, that until we have harvested many times the fruits of lives spent on earth, we will not, except in exceptional cases, live on higher planes beyond death.

Paul Beard suggests that "very unevolved men and women, with little spiritual understanding, are likely to be returned into incarnation very soon, simply because after death their perceptions cannot take them far. They have less scope. Being near to earth consciousness, they will return soon because they can learn better there. . . ." If souls are not sufficiently developed, they do not have the necessary spiritual awareness to cope with the higher spiritual levels.

We have the option to choose our parents and the circumstances of our next incarnation that will set the pattern of our lifetime on Earth. Many souls will choose their next incarnation during the *judgment stage*, a time when the soul becomes acutely aware of lessons still to be learned on Earth: patience, racial tolerance, humility and other soul enriching traits. All of these faults the soul sees clearly during the *judgment stage*.

Some souls need something besides an earthly incarnation for their further growth. Sally Lehmann, in 1958, reported on the birth into Earth of a child in whom she was interested "I was taken to the spheres . . . where souls are prepared for incarnation." There, she said, they were tested through a system of vibration to determine whether they could tolerate the vibrations of Earth. She saw "many lovely spirits tested and found unfit for earth and told to look elsewhere." When she asked her guide where they might go, the guide said, ". . . another planet, not quite so tense as earth."

Many wonder why we don't remember our past lives. In the Tenth Book of the *Republic,* Plato spoke of the choice returning souls have when they came to the River Lethe whose waters, when drunk, bring forgetfulness. Some drank more deeply and forgot all of their past lives, others who drank less, remembered some of their past lives.

In terms of the soul's growth, there are *practical* reasons for forgetting past incarnations. If we knew, for example, that we had lived one or more truly evil past lives, the staggering karmic debts to be repaid, personal entanglements to be resolved and the hard lessons to be learned, the knowledge might overwhelm us. This would lead to deep discouragement and despair.

The opposite could also be true. If we had been famous or a member of nobility or the ruling class in a previous incarnation, our ego and vanity could easily be a serious handicap to our spiritual growth. Our best course is to live each lifetime as lovingly and compassionately as we can, unhampered and unconcerned with our soul's past history.

Chapter Seven

Group Souls

ALL OF US know the experience of being instinctively drawn to someone for whom we have an immediate affinity and affection, even from the first time we meet them. There are many who automatically assume that this is a reunion with someone we have known in a previous life. Frances Banks went even further than that when she said that "souls who attract us are part of ourselves. They belong to the same group, the same spiritual family, the same group soul. Their connection with us is deeper and far more permanent than mere earth contacts could make it. . . ."

Most primary sources say that each of us have unconscious, but nonetheless strong spiritual attachments to a group of souls with whom we share collective aspirations. Members of soul groups live and act at various levels of spiritual maturity; while some still live on Earth, others of them live in the spirit world and can influence their lives on the unconscious, intuitive level.

Great artists, scientists and writers admit that inspiration for their important creative works comes from a source beyond themselves. Perhaps the best recorded account of how a group of souls in the spirit world inspired and directed the writing of a scholarly book is recorded in Raynor Johnson's *The Light and the Gate,* published in 1964. In it he recounts events that led him to write *Nurs-*

lings of Immortality. He depicts including how he became aware that he was part of a soul group which included Frederic Myers, who died in 1901, as well as one of Johnson's long-time friends, Ambrose Pratt, a well-known Australian mystic, scholar, naturalist and writer, who died in 1944.

Kindred souls on the other side can influence our unconscious minds with thoughts and ideas of which we are not consciously aware. Although they are invisible to us, they are no less alive than we are here. Johnson said he was never *consciously* aware of his group's help while writing *Nurslings of Immortality;* he nonetheless admitted that he had never before written with such a clear sense of mission. "It was," he said, "the most remarkable experience of my life."

Our relationship to other souls in our soul group is closer than we consciously aware and these relationships exist whether or not we are in the physical body. Ambrose Pratt, in a communication to Raynor Johnson, said that "souls of human beings travel in groups all interrelated but individualized on earth, they share a common unconsciousness."

Some group souls have only a few members while others have many thousands. They are guided by angels or other celestial beings as they help worthy causes and movements on Earth and carry out tasks of all different magnitudes, even missions which are planetary or cosmic in scope. Group souls may be interested in music, art, science, medicine, healing, literature, religion, social services or social sciences. Groups in the spirit world use dreams, visions, intuition and inspiration to influence their members who are on Earth. There are countless such soul groups.

Occasionally, while still serving and counselling newly arrived souls from Earth, Frances Banks visited higher planes in the company of a spiritually advanced soul with whom she worked on a receiving team. On one such visit, her guide explained the workings of soul groups and her own relationship to one such group. ". . . seek your place," he said, "ask that the light might open your mind to that which is for you; that your vibratory rate may be increased to respond to the vibration of your group; that you may become aware of them for they are close beside you. . . ."

Later, after she had earned the right to join her group, she said, "Every soul belongs to a group . . . one is part of the soul group as one is part of a family . . . a family relationship may be temporary but a soul relationship is eternal."

Light Magazine featured a dialogue between a group of English afterlife researchers and a discarnate who spoke with them, through a channel. This is what that person told them about the nature of soul groups.

> Group souls are in essence those to whom you are permanently attached; they are the spiritual frequency from which we are never separated, but which is generally beyond your range of hearing, just as certain sounds are beyond your range of hearing; so that to reach the

level of communication, you need to lift your own consciousness.

Paul Beard wrote in *Hidden Man* that members of a soul group, over many and various stages of incarnation, "work step by step, individually and in partnerships to achieve the long term purpose of the group. In the group soul there lies a deep aspect of true human belonging together, [of] life no longer as a battle but as companionship."

The knowledge that we not only survive, but also move in and out of incarnation in the company of our own soul family can be of great comfort as we approach the moment of transition. Still, death remains a great unknown. Facing death can be looked upon as a skill learned over many lifetimes and a greater understanding of our survival and our afterlife will shed new light on the opportunities - and the pitfalls - which will present themselves to us along the way.

Chapter Eight

An Other-Side View of Suicide

IN THIS TIME of widespread re-thinking of our attitudes towards life and death, living and dying, with the emergence of living wills and hospice care for the dying, it comes as no surprise that suicide is being given new consideration as well. The maxim of the Hemlock Society, for example, is "Good Life, Good Dying"; its philosophy makes it all too easy to believe that the avoidance of anticipated suffering by taking one's own life is a reasonable, even noble alternative to living and learning from one's suffering. Suicide can be made to sound quite relieving and practical, but how does it look from the other side, in light of the fact that we only die physically and our souls will incarnate again?

The question of whether suicide is a courageous or a cowardly act is not easily answered because we do not know the soul's past history or its karmic entanglements. All who commit suicide attempt to escape from what they believe, in their despair, to be insurmountable problems. But regardless of the circumstances, we never really escape the consequences of taking a life, even our own.

According to Frederic Myers, each suicide will face different kinds of consequences depending upon the character of the soul and the motive that precipitated the act.

There are exceptions - cases wherein the man who kills himself is filled with some noble purpose [and] sacrifices his life in order that, through his death, others may be relieved of want or of the painful sight of a loved one slowly perishing of an incurable disease . . . in some respects this "redeems him" from the suffering and anguish of others who selfishly committed suicide.

Rosamond Lehmann and Kathleen Raine reported on a man who, upon learning that he was terminally ill with cancer, shot himself. He saw it as he believed the ancient Greeks would have seen it - as an act of heroism. He was not going to be "taken by the enemy." His family was able to accept that he had "died a soldier's death" and this gave them strength. The discarnate source who spoke with Lehmann and Raine described how this was seen from the other side.

Because the family took it in that spirit, he had not injured them. However, he himself would still have to bear the equivalent of the physical pain he would have had to bear; because it could have been that this pain involved the opportunity to cancel a debt from another life by bearing it with valor and courage; it could be that by not facing it, he had left the debt unpaid. . . .

The main predicament of those who commit suicide, whether their motivation be selfish or unselfish, is that they have cut short or aborted a mission. Many of the consequences of suicide relate to having not completed a round of experience which was intended to be fulfilled on Earth. Taking one's own life is said to lead to a state of limited mobility on the other side. In contrast to persons who live out their lives, including their sufferings, and on the other side are able to move through the various stages of transition, those who commit suicide find themselves stranded. Tudor Pole remarked that they ". . . must expect to remain earth-bound at least until [their] natural span on earth would have been completed. In the meantime the condition of [their] existence in the shadow realm between earth and heaven will prove to be extremely difficult and unrewarding."

Many discarnate sources caution potential suicide victims against taking their lives and attempt to impress upon them that to be born on the Earth is always a special privilege; if that privilege is abused, they will have thrown away the special, personal purpose for which they have come onto this planet. By all accounts, committing suicide is a very foolish way to come to the other side. Such a soul comes back to Earth quickly, and throughout his or her new life will be confronted with many of the same problems.

What of those who are left behind by a loved one who decides to end his or her own life? A soul on the other side feels the effect of our thoughts and prayers; it is therefore important to bear in mind that our *attitude* toward the soul of that person makes a tremendous difference. There is agreement among all these sources that no matter how emotionally devastating the suicide of a loved one is, if we continue to say, "what a terrible thing to do" or "what a great shame to waste a life," it only adds to the victim's own shame, pain, and confusion. Frequent prayers invoking the Light of Christ to surround them is the best way to help them. All souls - regardless of how they have passed through transition - need our prayers. Indeed, we who remain on Earth can play a significant role in helping - or hindering - their progress toward release.

Chapter Nine

Grief, Tears and Prayers

SEPARATION

ONLY TIME can heal the trauma of separation, the isolation and loneliness facing those who survive the death of a loved one. It is important to realize that a stage of intense grieving is a necessary part of the mourning process; sadness and loneliness might continue for years. Tears and weeping through the night are natural and healthy, especially early on, because the suppression and delay of grief can be damaging to the inner life.

What does our grieving look like from the other side? Sally Lehmann warned that *prolonged*, undue grief restricts the natural progress of the departed soul. The strong psychic downward pull of bereaved survivors holds the sensitive soul near the Earth level longer than necessary. This needlessly keeps a soul tied to the Earth plane and restricts its freedom of passage to higher planes.

You must understand, a piece of me is always near you. It is as though I am free and exploring other states and dimensions, but a piece of me is with you. I know how you are feeling and when you are sending your love. . . . I can send serenity, and I can send protection and . . .

quietness when you need these things. . . . But for many people this is not the case at all. Either their families cease to think of them or they send such queer shut-in thoughts, full of grief and limitations. This causes great discomfort here, and we are in agony when some people hear the thoughts of their earth links. . . ."

RELEASE

Even for those who understand that protracted grief is often, in reality, self-pity and not a helpful way to express our love for the soul of our loved ones, the question remains: What can we do?

The distinction must be made between excessive grieving and concerted prayer for a soul's release. The kindest thing we can do for someone who has died is to pray immediately for the release of the soul from the Earth plane by asking that the Light of Christ surround and protect the soul from all influences that might impede its progress. The Catholic tradition of saying the rosary and burning candles for a departed soul is a helpful ritual for releasing and aiding the soul in its journey.

Despite the warnings of many discarnate communicators, there are those who attempt to contact loved ones on the other side either through automatic writing, ouija boards, or through novice psychics, activities which Tudor Pole says are not without far-reaching consequences.

There is considerable danger to [these] persons that forces of a chaotic, mischievous character may be unwittingly released through the unwise opening of such avenues, with results that can but prove deplorable. . . . This is a time for prayer and silence rather than for attempts to open doorways of communication between those who are in different states of consciousness.

The advice most frequently given is that survivors pray for the release and guidance of the departed soul on its way, although this may be difficult to do immediately after the death of a loved one. There are patterns which unfold in mourning, however, as we shift from non-acceptance to acceptance. An example of one type of scenario would be that of a mother or father who grieves for years over the death of a young child. The grieving parent might begin to have recurring dreams in which the child is seen sitting alone on the bank of a river or some other body of water which separates her from a group of happy children who are playing on the other side. The time might come when the parents relate all this to a wise friend and are told that the dream is probably trying to *tell* them something: their grief and tears are being symbolized by the river which is keeping their daughter from joining the other children on the other side. Finally, when they begin to pray for their daughter's release, the recurring dream ends.

Many Christians pray for those who are sick, but cease their prayers after the patient dies. The first two weeks after death, however, are especially important time to pray for the departed soul. Prayers help to lessen the soul's fears and anxieties as it becomes adjusted to its new world.

Recalling the first stage of transition, the *call*, described in Chapter Two, another helpful way in which survivors can help the dying patient is to invoke, by name, some of the patient's friends and loved ones, who are already on the other side, asking them to be there when the soul arrives. This is especially important when the dying person does not believe in survival, or may be too confused to call for help.

Flowers, prayers and kind thoughts are more helpful to departed souls than many people realize. Many of our funeral and burial customs reflect, albeit largely unconsciously, an understanding of this. In his book *A Vision of the Aquarian Age,* Sir George Trevelyan commented on this.

> The ritual of lying in state for two or three days has profound meaning, for the soul during this time often hovers around its former habitation, getting accustomed to leaving it. There are many descriptions of how the "dead" person finds himself floating discarnate above his own body. Such descriptions establish the importance of flowers around the coffin. . . . The astral and etheric bodies are drawn by the flowers and

lights, and the process of transition is made gentler. The very stillness and dignity of the milieu aids the soul to free itself.

Chapter Ten

Facing Death
In the Light of Survival

"The beauty which the artist tried to capture, but eluded him; the music which haunted the musician but could not be expressed; the love which flowed between two souls whom fate parted. The child whose life closed before it had scarcely begun; the unfinished symphonies of human life are not lost or blown by the winds of time. They are precious to the Father in whose keeping they remain and they will be given back in perfection at the close of the journey."

Raynor Johnson

EVEN THOSE WHO BELIEVE IN SURVIVAL and do not fear death itself, feel anxiety about the almost inevitable suffering that precedes dying. It is impossible to pretend that this phase is easy, and yet, the manner in which we pass through it is of tremendous significance. We can either face this suffering with bitterness and anger and add nothing to our spiritual development, or we can convert this final stage of suffering into spiritual growth. It is possible to react with grace and an acceptance of our situation that moves us a giant step forward along the spiritual path. Our attitudes and reactions to any unavoidable suffering we bear determines the degree of spiritual good that we gain.

Viktor Frankl, the Viennese psychiatrist who developed logotherapy, expressed this idea, saying that "human life can be fulfilled not only in creating and enjoying, but also in suffering. Life . . . can receive its ultimate meaning not only as a result of death . . ., but in the very process of death. Not only the sacrifice of one's life can give meaning; life can reach nobility even as it flounders on the rocks."

This profound truth is exceedingly difficult to recognize in the midst of suffering and despair. Yet somehow, numberless unknown souls have the will and fortitude to face it with uncompromising faith. An eloquent example was related to Raynor Johnson, by the English Clergyman, Dr. Leslie Weatherhead, whose sister wrote these words just a few days before she died.

Father, I do not ask that Thou shouldst always save me from trouble. I know that Thou wilt [allow] nothing come upon me beyond what, in Thy strength, I can bear. But I ask, rather, that in every new experience I may know that Thou art with me and that I may not miss the gift hidden in the heart of every pain. Thou hast cast my lot in this strange, hard time. Teach me so to carry myself through these days . . . that I may win from them a firmer hold on Thee and a new power to bring to others of Thy needy children, the comfort of Thy love.

Her deep faith in God's will and ultimate justice and mercy gave her the necessary strength to face the supreme test. By accepting her fate bravely with undiminished faith, she reached a new milestone of spirituality, a new level of spiritual maturity that elevated her to a high spiritual plane in the next world.

Paul Beard, in a recent letter to me about illness and suffering, told of a friend, a former dancer, who spent the last two years completely paralyzed and unable to talk. When he contacted her after her death she told him, referring to this time of suffering, "oh, I cannot tell you how worthwhile it was."

There are some who do not believe it is God's will that they suffer, but nevertheless face their death with courage. They know that their suffering is linked to the misuse of their own free will in some past life. In both cases, however, it was their strong faith in a divine order that carried them through.

Some patients, when told that they have terminal cancer, follow the frequent pattern of shock, denial, anger, bargaining, depression and acceptance. Others, after a short period of adjustment, reach the stage of acceptance without anger and depression. They rise quickly to a new level of awareness, a new plane of consciousness that allows them to see beauty they have never seen before. Each new sunset, each flower, each wonder of nature, becomes a thing of beauty and each day a new gift to savor. They become keenly aware of small acts of kindness and love as they move slowly toward the door of the next world.

97

HOSPICE

The weeks and months that immediately precede death can be emotionally and spiritually devastating. Both believers and non-believers come to a point where they need to share their physical, mental and spiritual burdens. Only through sharing can they lessen their pain, their fears, loneliness and anxiety. With each passing week, the patient's emotional, physical and spiritual needs become increasingly acute. Yet this is often precisely the time when the quality of concern and attention shown by doctors, nurses and friends seems to diminish.

Medical professionals can easily feel that they have "lost the battle," with the result that they now feel unable to sustain the intensity of interest and challenge to help heal the patient's psyche. Even friends and relatives become unsure of what to say or do and begin, more and more, to leave the patient alone.

Hospice volunteers who work with patients play a vital role at this point. They are third parties who can demonstrate to the patient that someone cares. They are there because they want to be and their patients sense this. This willingness to show compassion by sharing the patient's fears and concerns is deeply comforting and reassuring.

If there is ever a time when a human being needs to share his or her feelings honestly, it is the period preceding death. Many times, the hospice volunteers are the ones who provide the miracle of peace and understanding to the dying patient, which makes that important sharing possible. A unique kind of psychic exchange occurs, sometimes in silence, by just being present, giving love and compassion. In turn, love flows from the patient back to the volunteer. Both the patient and the volunteer experience a new sense of worth and a new stage of spiritual growth.

CONCLUSION

DEATH IS A TRANSITION into a fuller expression of love and life. The process of dying is our passage into that new realm. Embracing this reality begins when we face up to the fact that this earthly life is transitory. The dying person has been made acutely aware of what is true for each of us: we are mortal. We are all in a terminal condition. Our process of dying, death itself and the afterlife are part and parcel of our humanity; they belong to our wholeness.

Suffering increases when a person feels diminished in his or her worth as a human being, when some element of that wholeness is compromised or denied. A dying person is on the verge of emerging as a free soul in a new dimension of consciousness, and it makes an immense difference if caregivers recognize this. Hospice volunteers find that if a patient is given adequate physical care and enough human companionship much of the anguish of dying can be relieved. By the time that hospice volunteers enter into the picture, this spiritual emergence has become the central event in that person's life, around which all else turns.

Dying persons desperately need to be assured, right up to the very end, of their worth, and this must include respect for the momentous process which is unfolding in them. This book is dedicated to a better understanding of that process in the hope that through it, the reader may take comfort in the knowledge that life is continuous and that, though we die to the life of this world, we are also reborn into ever-greater opportunities for growth, service and joy.

ABOUT THE AUTHOR

IT IS NOT ALWAYS POSSIBLE to separate a book from its author and still have the same book. The two are joined at the hip in an unequal symbiosis. The author might live quite well without the book, but the book cannot live a full life without its author. This is especially true as we move along the continuum of reading matter toward books which are generated out of the author's intensely personal experiences and beliefs.

Death Without Fear is this kind of book because in it Harvey Humann presents material which changed his own life. He finished *Death Without Fear* during the last year of his life, which spanned the core years of this century. This book, his second, is one of the fruits of a long and thoughtful involvement with the processes of death and dying and research into what takes place after death.

Harvey Humann's life was marked by what we Americans like to call "the frontier experience," although the frontiers changed many times during his life. He was born on the edge of North America's natural vastness, but he died on the edge of a very different kind of frontier.

He was named after the town of Harvey, North Dakota, where he was born April 8, 1908 as one of the eleven children of Henry Humann, a Seventh Day Adventist minister, and Katherine Reiswig Humann. This was also the year that Harvey Humann's father was invited by land developers to inspect a vast tract of virgin prairie which had become available for settlement outside of Calgary in Alberta, Canada. Overwhelmed by what he saw, the elder Humann returned to his flock and persuaded a handful of families to move, in spite of the coming winter, to this "Promised Land." We can only guess, but there is every indication that this trek of 900 miles was undertaken with a sense of urgency, in the belief that in this way they were somehow promoting the coming of the Kingdom of God, hastening the Return of Christ.

Education was taken seriously by the Humann family and Harvey completed degrees in both Philosophy and English at the University of Nebraska. It was 1933, the same year that he and his wife, Audrey, were married. A series of teaching jobs led the Humanns to Kansas City where Harvey trained one Summer in the processing of quartz crystals with the Crystal Products Company. The industrial use of quartz was in its infancy, but even then it was considered vital to the war effort, which meant a deferment for Harvey who was by that time a manager at Crystal Products. Following the war, he owned a number of small businesses before returning in 1951 to Kansas City. There, he became involved again with quartz production and the relatively new field of manufactured synthetic quartz with the Electro-Dynamics Company of Mission, Kansas, which thrived during the heyday of the mass-production of automobiles and television. He was president of the company for five years before retiring in 1983.

The "paper trail" of Humann's involvement with afterlife research leads back to the 1950's when he began reading Sherwood Eddy, Gina Cerminara, Thomas Sugrue and Edgar Cayce. Cayce's son, Hugh Lynn, spoke in Kansas City in the 1960's and provided Humann with a new personal opening to the subjects of the afterlife and reincarnation. Humann soon became active in the Association for Research and Enlightenment (Edgar Cayce Foundation) for which he organized study groups and lectured all around the country, later becoming a member of the organization's Long-Range Planning Committee and the Board of Trustees.

In 1970, when the A.R.E. invited Raynor Johnson, Chancellor of Queen's College in Melbourne, Australia and an acknowledged expert on the afterlife, to speak at Unity Village in Lee's Summit, Missouri, Harvey Humann was on hand and the encounter between the two men led to a lasting friendship. It was Harvey Humann who introduced Raynor Johnson to Paul Beard, who then arranged for Johnson to address the College of Psychic Studies in London, of which he was President.

If there was a single factor which joined Harvey Humann's interest in the afterlife with his outer activity, it was his work with hospice patients. In the late 1970's, he became involved with the development of Hospice Care of Mid-America Hospice and was Chairman of the Board of the organization after his retirement from Electro-Dynamics in 1983. In 1983, he received the Service to Hospice Care Award and in 1981, he and Audrey received the Kansas City Service Foundation Award for Outstanding Volunteer Achievement.

His first book, *The Many Faces of Angels,* now in its third printing, was published in 1986 and numerous

105

articles by Harvey Humann on spiritual growth and the afterlife have appeared in A.R.E. publications. Harvey Humann died at home in Lawrence, Kansas in October of 1990. He was 82 years old.

Annotated Bibliography

THIS BIBLIOGRAPHY IS INTENDED to serve as a resource for the interested reader who wishes to explore the vast body of literature about the survival of bodily death and life after this major transition. It contains, in addition to sources quoted in *Death Without Fear*, an extended listing of book titles by authors represented in this book, including a brief introductory sketch of several of these authors without whose work this book could never have been written. The author wishes to express his heartfelt thanks to each of them.

FRANCES BANKS (see Helen Greaves)

PAUL BEARD, leading English psychical researcher, has been a participating member of the English Society of Psychical Research for 40 years. His books have become classics in the field. For 16 years he was President of the College of Psychic Studies, London.

Beard, Paul, (Ed.), *The Barbanell Report*, Pilgrim Books, Tasburgh, Norwich, England, 1987.

Beard, Paul, *Hidden Man*, Pilgrim Books, Tasburgh, Norwich, England, 1986.

Beard, Paul, *Living On*, George Allen & Unwin Ltd., Ruskin House, 40 Museum Street, London, W.C. 1, England, 1980.

Beard, Paul, (Ed.), *The James-John Experiment*, (C.P.S. Paper No.6), College of Psychic Studies Ltd., 16 Queensberry Place, London S.W.7., 1973.

Beard, Paul, *Survival of Death*, Hodder and Stoughton Ltd., St. Paul's House, Warwick Lane, London, E.C.4., England, 1966.

EDGAR CAYCE, (1877-1945), was the best-known American Christian mystic, seer and clairvoyant. Between 1901 and 1945, he gave over 14,000 clairvoyant readings, including 2,500 life readings that testified to man's many incarnations on Earth and other planets, and 9,000 readings for patients who sought his help for physical ailments, plus hundreds of spiritual discourses on the nature of man and his relationship to God. All readings are computerized for study in the A.R.E. Library, Virginia Beach, Virginia.

HUGH LYNN CAYCE (1907-1982) was the son of Edgar Cayce and wrote extensively in the field of psychic studies. For thirty years, he led the A.R.E.

CONTACT: A.R.E., Inc.
67th Street and Atlantic Ave.
P.O. Box 595
Virginia Beach, VA 23451

DR. GINA CERMINARA, *Many Mansions,* William Sloane Associates, Inc, New York, NY, 1950.

GRACE COOKE is the channel for the teachings of White Eagle, whose mission was "to spread the great carpet of peace and brotherhood in the world."

White Eagle books by Grace Cooke:
Gentle Brother   *Golden Harvest*
Path of the Soul   *Quiet Mind*
Prayer in the New Age   *Morning Light*
Living Word of St. John   *Way of the Sun*
Jesus, Teacher and Healer   *Still Voice*
Wisdom from White Eagle
Spiritual Unfoldment, Volumes I, II, III, IV
See also *The Return of Arthur Conan Doyle*, edited by Ivan Cooke.

CONTACT: White Eagle Lodge,
            9, St. Mary Abbots Place,
            London, W.8.,
            England

DR. ROBERT CROOKALL was a lecturer in Botany at the University of Aberdeen and principal geologist at H. M. Geological Survey in London.

Crookall, Robert, *The Supreme Adventure*, Carol Publishing Group, 600 Madison Avenue, New York, NY 10022, (1961).

GERALDINE CUMMINS, Irish born sensitive and author of *The Road to Immortality* and *Beyond Human Personality*. The contents of both books are purported to have been communicated to her by Frederick Myers (see note on page 101).

Cummins, Geraldine, *Beyond Human Personality*, Ivor Nicholson & Watson, Limited, London, 1935.

Cummins, Geraldine, *The Road to Immortality*, Pilgrims Book Services, Tasburgh, Norwich England. First published in 1932, Abridged Edition, 1984.

Cummins, Geraldine, *Travellers in Eternity*, Psychic Press Ltd., 144 High Holborn, London, W.C.1., England, 1948.

VIKTOR E. FRANKL, M.D., *The Doctor and the Soul - From Psychotherapy to Logotherapy*, Vintage Books, Random House, New York, NY, 1973.

HELEN GREAVES, English sensitive and author of *The Dissolving Veil* and *Testimony of Light* which consisted of thirty-eight telepathic messages from the discarnate mind of Frances Banks. Banks was formerly the Anglican Sister Mary of the Community of the Resurrection, Grahamstown, South Africa. For 25 years, she was a Sister and Principal of the Teacher's Training College of Grahamstown and author of *Frontiers of Revelation,* a treatise on mysticism, and *Teach Them to Live,* based on her experiences as a counselor at Maidstone Gaol Prison in England. Frances Banks died in 1965.

Greaves, Helen, *Testimony of Light* (1969) and *The Dissolving Veil* (1967), originally published by The World Fellowship Press Ltd.

Banks Frances, *Four Studies in Mysticism* (1967), The World Fellowship Press, Ltd.

CONTACT: C.W. Daniel Co.,
1 Church Path,
Saffron Walden,
Essex, ENGLAND

RAYNOR JOHNSON (1901-1987) was lecturer in physics at the University of Belfast from 1923 to 1927, lecturer in physics at the University of London, King's College from 1927 to 1934, and in the years from 1935 until 1964, he was Master of Queens College in Melbourne, Australia.

Johnson, Raynor, *The Imprisoned Splendour* (1953), *Nurslings of Immortality* (1957), *Watcher on the Hills* (1959), *Light and the Gate* (1964), *A Pool of Reflection* (1975) all published by Hodder and Stoughton Limited, St. Paul's House, Warwick Lane, London, E.C.4., England.

Johnson, Raynor, *Religious Outlook for Modern Man*, McGraw-Hill Book Co., 330 West 42nd Street, New York, NY 10036, 1963.

111

Johnson, Raynor, *Psychical Research - Exploring the Supernatural*, Funk and Wagnals, 1968.

Johnson, Raynor, *The Spiritual Path*, Harper and Row, 49 East 33rd Street, New York, NY 10016, 1971.

ELISABETH KÜBLER-ROSS, M.D. has long been regarded as the world's foremost expert on death and dying. Her book, *On Death and Dying,* was a bestseller and was followed by a long list of books which have become standard reading in this field.

Books by Dr. Kübler-Ross include
On Death and Dying, MacMillan, 866 Third Avenue, New York, NY, 10022 , 1969;
Questions and Answers on Death and Dying, MacMillan, New York, NY, 1974;
Living With Death and Dying, MacMillan, New York, NY, 1981;
Death: The Final Stage of Growth, Prentice-Hall, Englewood Cliffs, NJ, 1975;
On Children and Death, MacMillan, New York, NY, 1983;
Working it Through, MacMillan, New York, NY, 1982
AIDS: The Ultimate Challenge, MacMillan, New York, NY, 1987.

ROSAMOND LEHMANN, prominent novelist and regular contributor to *Light* Magazine of which she was also an editorial board member. Her book, *Swan in the Evening* tells of her most important mystical and psychical experiences. She compiled, together with Cynthia Sandys, a series of "letters," messages from Lehmann's two daughters who died in 1957 and 1958.

Lehmann, Rosamond, *Swan in the Evening,* William Collins Ltd.

Lehmann, Rosamond, *Letters From our Daughters - Parts 1 and 2,* The College of Psychic Studies, 16 Queensberry Place, London S.W.7., England, 1970.

JOSEPH LEEMING, *Yoga and the Bible*, Radha Soami Satsang Beas, Punjab, India.

LIGHT MAGAZINE, the quarterly of The College of Psychic Studies, 16 Queensberry Place, London S.W.7., England. *Light* first appeared on January 8th, 1881, which predates the founding of The College of Psychic Studies, which was founded in 1884 as an educational charity to foster free inquiry into the fields of psychical and afterlife research.

RAYMOND MOODY'S study in the early 1970's of over one hundred cases of persons who had been "clinically dead" and then revived was reported in his 1975 book, *Life After Life.* Although a good deal of clinical documentation about the near-death experience existed before Moody's work, *Life After Life* was among the very first publications to place these findings before the general public.

Moody, Raymond, *Life After Life*, Mockingbird Books, Inc., P.O. Box 110, Covington, GA 30209, 1975.

Moody, Raymond, *Reflections on Life After Life*, Bantam Books, 666 Fifth Ave., New York, NY 10019.

FREDERIC W. H. MYERS (1843-1901) was a distinguished classical scholar and Fellow of Trinity College in Cambridge. He was a scholar, poet and the author of numerous essays which reflected his interest in the systematic investigation of parapsychological phenomena. He was the leader of a small group who, in 1882, founded the Society for Psychical Research.

Myers, Frederick, *Human Personality and its Survival of Bodily Death*, Ayer Co. Publishers, P.O. Box 958, Salem, NH 03079, originally published by Longmans, Green and Co., Chicago, 1937.

ALBERT PAUCHARD (1878-1934) was a long-time President of the Psychic Studies Institute in Geneva. *The Other Side* is a record of his telepathic messages to his sister, recorded in writing by "M.J."

Pauchard, Albert, *The Other World*, The College of Psychic Studies Ltd., 16 Queensberry Place, London, S.W.2., 1952, this selection published, 1973.

W. TUDOR POLE (1884-1968) was an archaeologist, philosopher, seer and healer. In 1940, at the time of the Battle of Dunkirk, he founded the Big Ben Silent Minute, endorsed by King George VI and Winston Churchill. When Big Ben tolled nine o'clock, all of London stood silent to pray for peace and protection. In 1959, Pole established the Chalice Well Trust in Glastonbury, Somerset, England. His books were originally published by Neville Spearman Ltd.

Pole, W. Tudor, *The Silent Road* (1960), *A Man Seen From Afar*, C.W. Daniel Co., 1 Church Path, Saffron Walden, Essex, England for The Chalice Well Trust.

Pole, W. Tudor, *Writing in the Ground,* Pilgrim Books, Tasburgh, Norwich, England, 1968.

KATHLEEN RAINE, poet and Blake scholar, has been regular contributor to *Light Magazine*, the periodical of the College of Psychic Studies, 16 Queensberry Place, London, SW7, 2EB, England.

KENNETH RING, *Heading Toward Omega*, William Morrow and Company, 105 Madison Avenue, New York, NY 10016, 1985.

MICHAEL SABOM, *Recollections of Death: A Medical Investigation*, Harper and Row, 49 East 33rd Street, New York, NY 10016, 1984.

RUDOLF STEINER, *Life Between Death and Rebirth*, Anthroposophic Press, Bell's Pond, Star Route, Hudson, New York, NY 12534, 1968.

THOMAS SUGRUE, *There is a River*, Holt, Rinehart and Winston, 383 Madison Avenue, New York, NY 10017, 1973.

EMANUEL SWEDENBORG (1688-1772), was a Swedish engineer, mathematician and scientist. At the age of 59, he retired to devote his time to the interpretation of his dreams and the messages which came to him with increasing frequency from spiritual beings. At the time of his death in 1772, he had published 16 books, including a private spiritual diary of five volumes. His major book was *Heaven and Hell*.

Swedenborg, Emanuel, *Heaven and Hell*, Swedenborg Foundation, Inc., 139 East 23rd Street, New York, NY 10010.

RUTH MATTSON TAYLOR is the editor of after-death communications from the noted theologian A.D. Mattson through the English clairvoyant Margaret Flavell Tweddell.

Taylor, Ruth, *Witness From Beyond*, Foreword Books, 11 Graffam Road, South Portland, Maine 04106, 1975, 1977, 1980.

SIR GEORGE TREVELYAN founded of the Wrekin Trust in 1971, a non-profit organization dedicated to the promotion of spiritual development and the ongoing exchange between science and mysticism. Sir George is probably best known internationally for his leading role in the Lamplighter Movement.

Trevelyan, George, *A Vision of the Aquarian Age*, Sigo Press, 25 New Chardon Street, #8748, Boston, MA 02114, 1984.